THE COMPLETE

SEARCH COMMITTEE

GUIDEBOOK

An Executive Recruiter
Leads You Step-by-Step Through the
Process of Finding God's Person for
Your Church or Organization

ROBERT W. DINGMAN

GL
Regal Books
A Division of GL Publications
Ventura, California, U.S.A.

Published by Regal Books
A Division of GL Publications
Ventura, California 93006
Printed in U.S.A.

Library of Congress Cataloging-in-Publication Data

Dingman, Robert W., 1926-
 The complete search committee guidebook for choosing the right leader /
Robert W. Dingman.
  p.   cm.
 Bibliography: p.
 ISBN: 0-8307-1265-8
 1. Pastoral search committees.   I. Title.
BV664.D56   1989
254—dc20
                                                        89-34068
                                                        CIP

1 2 3 4 5 6 7 8 9 10 / 91 90 89

Rights for publishing this book in other languages are contracted by Gospel
Literature International (GLINT) foundation. GLINT also provides technical
help for the adaptation, translation, and publishing of Bible study resources
and books in scores of languages worldwide. For further information, contact
GLINT, Post Office Box 488, Rosemead, California, 91770, U.S.A., or the
publisher.

CONTENTS

A NOTE OF APPRECIATION

MANY pastors, presidents of colleges and leaders of parachurch organizations assisted me as I labored to write this book. They and their wives are a pretty talented group, which is why I contacted them. To gain perspective, I also needed to know about the average and even the untalented, whom I learned about through others. I am indebted to them all, though more to some than others.

Rev. Roger Meriwether, my own pastor, inspired me to care about what happens to those who are our undershepherds. Also, growing up in a minister's home helped some.

Earl Roe, my editor, was very supportive to this first-time writer, and I appreciate his patience. Donna Hustace, my research assistant, provided valuable help while living her own busy life. Connie Morley was my strong right arm in organizing the material and preparing it. I owe much to her.

Most of all, my thanks to Jan, my wife of 37 years. My writing frequently frayed her patience as I tried to fit this project into our already busy lives. Hon, I promise never to write another book. Thanks for hanging in there.

INTRODUCTION

W IIO should read this book?

If you are concerned about or involved in the process of selecting a leader for a church, a parachurch organization or a college, seminary or Bible school, then you are the person I wrote this book for. This guidebook on choosing the right leaders for God's people is a practical handbook designed to guide a search committee through the tedious and complicated process of finding a new leader.

If you have ever read a book on redecorating your house or on repairing your VW, you already know something about "how to" books. But unlike those books, our "how to" is concerned with groups of people, with things of the Spirit, with the leading of God and with understanding how a religious community can grow and prosper under good leadership.

The Primary Users

This book will be helpful to any search committee appointed to find the next leader for its group.

Churches. The majority of churches are self-governing; that is, structured to find their own leaders, with varying degrees of help or direction from their denominations, if they are in one. They will find valuable guidance here.

Admittedly, in religios bodies with centralized authority, such as the United Methodist Church, the Roman Catholic Church and the Salvation Army, they assign their clergy to various posts. Yet even within these groups, various posts such as directors of Christian education or ministers of music—are filled following intensive searches for the appropriate leadership personnel. This book speaks directly to the concerns of these search committees as well.

Educational Institutions and Parachurch Groups. When faced with a need for a change in leadership, the chairperson of the board of an educational institution, relief ministry, missions organization and the like will also find this book useful as the process begins in the search for a new leader.

Professional Search Personnel. Seminaries, Bible Schools and denominations have people appointed to assist churches as they seek new pastors. For them also, this handbook will prove helpful.

The Point of View
The language and frame of reference I use will be most comfortable and familiar for the reader who is from the sector of the religious spectrum called "evangelical Christian." "Fundamentalist" groups, if there is a meaningful distinction, will also find it congenial in tone and spirit. This point of view is used because this is who I am and where I am at.

However, the material can be useful to a much larger group of readers if they do not find the language and frame of reference troublesome. I believe Jewish congregations can also use this book in selecting a new rabbi for their temple or synagogue because the procedures outlined are broadly applicable.

The Author's Credentials
A discerning reader will begin with a questioning of the credentials of the author. Examining the writer's claim to having expertise in any field is a good starting point for a reader.

Since 1961, I have served as a consultant in the executive
search profession. The prior 10 years were spent in industry,
education and government, working in personnel management
roles. For over 30 years, I have been involved in the functions of
employment and recruiting, primarily in the world of business
and industry. In recent years, my own executive search practice
has focused on filling positions only at senior management levels.

In the religious world, I have had the privilege of assisting 10
evangelical Christian parachurch organizations in their quest for
new presidents or executive directors. These bodies vary from
overseas agencies—quite large global ministries and others
serving only in Japan or Africa—to those operating primarily in
the U.S.A.

Lastly, as you are probably doing now if you've read this far, I
have served on the pastoral selection committees of churches
where I have worshiped, as well as on other committees
charged with finding a youth minister or a minister of music. I
think you will agree that I have paid my dues.

Is the Author a Sexist?

It's said to be bad form these days to use words, concepts or
illustrations that cast men and women in different roles or imply
that persons of either gender cannot be equally gifted in whatever role is being discussed. Hopefully motherhood and father-
hood are exceptions to this rationale.

Let me state for the record that in this book "he" could just
as easily be "she." I have read more than enough on the quality
of women leaders to know that my choice of using only masculine pronouns will offend some readers who will see this practice
as unfair. Yet I have chosen not to resort to the silly, if equaliz-
ing, device of "he/she" or other such contrivances to placate
those sensitive to this matter. This is my first writing venture,
so be gracious to me, please, and do not put that particular burden on me. Thanks.

Aren't there any women Christian leaders? Sure there are.
But, so far, not many. The traditional view is that our Old Testament heritage set a cultural stage for us of leaders who are

almost all masculine. Yes, I remember Esther, but my point is still valid. Even New Testament writings don't provide many female leader role models for today's Church.

Given the reliance of so many churches on traditional interpretations of Scripture for shaping their leadership and that of parachurch organizations, it is not surprising that women still are quite uncommon as leaders in the Christian community. The controversy rages on about female religious leadership, and I, for one, find the defense of the male status quo by old men as tiresome as the overly strident calls for equal treatment by bright and aggressive women.

This book will not consider the selection of female candidates per se, because at this point the vast majority of senior leadership roles for Christian groups—the focus of this book—still involves men. A notable exception is the 1987 selection of Dr. Roberta Hestenes as president of Eastern College. She also serves as chair of the board of World Vision.

If you have a bias on the subject, I doubt that anything I could say would cause you to alter it in any way, so I won't try. However, if you are a little curious about my views on the subject, I will leave you with this question to ponder: If God gave us our various gifts to be used to honor Him and to be used in His kingdom, why did He bother to give so many women the intelligence, the ability to develop a deeply spiritual walk, plus excellent communicating and relational skills, if they were not to share in the leadership task?

CHAPTER ONE
"WE NEED A NEW PASTOR"

HELLO, George. This is Bill. I'm glad I caught you at home this evening. I'm calling on church business because something of major importance came as a surprise to me today. Pastor Johnson came to see me at my office this afternoon and said that, at the church board meeting next week, he plans to announce his resignation."

George was stunned. "You must be kidding, Bill. He's been with us 12 years, things are going fairly well and he's 51 years old. Why would he want to leave? This will be a big blow to the church. What do we do now?"

Bill had been thinking hard about the matter ever since the pastor's visit that afternoon, and he replied. "As board chairman, I'll have to spend a lot of time overseeing the running of the church. So I'm asking you, George, to chair the search committee to find us a new pastor. It's the most important task we have at this point, and I think you would be the best person to do it. I do need you for this job, George, so I hope you'll take it."

Before George could respond, Bill continued. "Could you join me for lunch tomorrow, so I can tell you what's involved? You'll want to talk to Betsy about it, of course, before you give me your answer. But I'd like your decision in two days, so we can be ready to announce your appointment right after Pastor gives the board the bad news."

George agreed to meet for lunch and Bill breathed a sigh of relief as he added, "Thanks, friend, for considering this assignment. The entire church will be in your debt if you do serve as our search committee chairman. See you in the office at 12 tomorrow. Good night, George."

The Leadership Selection Problem

That kind of call happens thousands of times each year. Churches around the world repeat this experience, as do Christian colleges, Bible schools and parachurch organizations. In most cases, the George involved asks himself, "What is involved with running the pastoral selection committee and how would we go about finding a new pastor?"

The answers to that question are provided in this book. The process is fairly logical but takes a lot of time and effort to do well. As with most things, there are the tricks of the trade that need to be learned if you are going to be successful. This book seeks to provide you with the plan, the process and the techniques that are needed.

In Days of Yore

A sense of perspective can often be helpful, so let's start with a historical overview.

Religious leadership was at its simplest and was most efficient when God spoke directly to His individual followers. When He spoke to Adam or Abraham, the only problems were those of obedience. When Moses was appointed Israel's leader, God spoke mostly to this man who then carried His messages to the nation.

A lot of problems developed between Moses and the Israelites, but they didn't have to choose their own leader. God had done that for them, and at times they wished He hadn't bothered

Great Moments in Church History: "Because we've always done it that way!" is said for the first time in a board meeting.

Source: *Leadership,* Winter 1988, p. 30. Reprinted by permission of Ron Wheeler.

to do it. That's the pattern of Old Testament leadership selection. God did it for His people, whether in the form of a king or a judge. And at times He even allowed unbelievers to rule them to get some points across to a proud and disobedient nation.

By New Testament times, Jesus was selecting His 12 disciples, and after His death the Apostle Paul slipped into leadership by the side door. When Paul took his missionary journeys and set up small groups of believers wherever he went, the Church faced the problem of where to find leadership. The churches were new, the converts untrained and the primary theological training was Paul's letters. The leadership was appointed by Paul, Barnabas and Titus, according to Scripture. An insight of the early Church gained from the New Testament reveals that the worship services were patterned after those of Jewish synagogues. So was their practice of local self-government.

Today this congregational form of church government has been reestablished after hundreds of years of centralized authority under the Catholic Church. With Luther and the Reformation came a renewal of self-governing churches, and today most Protestant churches are such, with varying levels of direction from the church hierarchy if it is denominationally related. The United Methodists and the Salvation Army represent groups that use a centralized authority.

The Most Important Task

The function of a church is to assist the members both in their worship of God and in proclaiming the good news. Perhaps the most important single act for the congregation is the selection of a leader. This fact is no less true for the parachurch organization or the educational institution.

Only the most uninterested church member will fail to participate in the selection of a new pastor. The pastoral selection process will hopefully involve every member, and it is a time for everyone to seek God's leading and exercise their own judgment as to whether the candidate meets with their approval. As at no other time in the life of the congregation, full participation is needed because of the far-reaching consequences of the action they will be taking.

What is the single act most closely related to the growth or success of a church or educational institution?

The choice of the leader.

What is the most closely associated with the failure of these same groups?

The choice of the leader.

Very few groups can rise higher than the abilities and inspiration of their leader. God seems to work then through human leadership of groups of believers. This makes the leadership selection task of crucial importance, does it not?

Varying Gifts

Scripture is quite clear that God gave gifts of a differing nature to various believers (see Eph. 4:11-13 and 1 Cor. 12:4-11). I believe that God expects you to know what gifts are needed to effectively minister to your group and to go find such a person. Both Scripture and our own experience tells us that no person has all the needed skills with nice balance, so it is essential to put in the needed learning and effort to seek out the person best equipped to meet your needs.

New Testament writers lived in a simpler age and some of today's problems did not exist. Congregations were small and no mention is made of the talents needed to raise funds, to oversee a building program or to develop a multifaceted program with good music, Christian education and a strong missions effort. Today we find "management" to be an increasingly important word but it is not a biblical term.

Today very few churches can afford to have as a pastor someone who is only a good proclaimer. Perhaps only the very large church can afford to do so, where there is an executive pastor backing up the communicator and running things. Today's churches of several hundred or more require team ministry where close cooperation of a staff is essential.

Each year, many failures occur in Christian leadership and the reasons are varied. The conspicuous Bakker and Swaggart cases, I suggest, are the exceptions, thank the Lord! More commonly, such failure is because of a bad selection in the first place.

This knowledge reaffirms the absolute importance of conducting the selection process carefully and of knowing what you are doing.

To go through a search process and still to have a bad result is easier than you might think. Usually this happens when a search committee does not look deeply enough within to see what the needs are and then to look carefully at candidates who offer those skills. If your search committee carefully reads this

---

The leader you select should offer compelling evidence that he has the relational skills, vision and caring for people that will allow him to lead your church, college or parachurch group effectively.

---

book and follows the procedures it outlines, the likelihood of a poor result will be greatly reduced.

The High Price of Poor Leadership

A good preacher can also be a poor leader, as we all realize. It then seems strange that so many churches seem to view preaching skills as the primary criterion in their search and fail to look at broader leadership abilities as at least as important. Leadership cannot be exercised without followers, and the leader you select should offer compelling evidence that he has the relational skills, vision and caring for people that will allow him to lead your church, college or parachurch group effectively.

Those who are devoid of leadership abilities are easily detected, if you carefully inquire into their background. Such detection is a problem for a search committee only when you are considering someone who has no track record as a leader. The recent seminary graduate applying for his first church is such an example or the college professor who is moving directly into the management role of president.

Those lacking significant leadership skills usually become aware of it and seek productive roles where it is not needed. Writers, evangelists, musicians, teachers, fund-raisers, translators, pilots, doctors and nurses and many other varieties of ministry opportunities allow such people to have satisfying and significant careers without leadership skills.

Then what *is* the problem for the search committee as it seeks to avoid poor leadership? A person's ministry can have some outstanding periods as well as some less productive ones. Some start off slowly and build well to a high point as they conclude their career. Others have a fast takeoff, flame out and crash. Your task is to see where the candidate is now in his faith pilgrimage and the evolution of his career.

Several prominent television evangelists' careers went down in flames during 1987-88. Your search committee must try to sense whether a candidate's ego needs, spiritual depth, life-style and vision of ministry holds a serious future peril. It is a difficult task to try to find such answers.

Some distinguished, but less-visible, Christian leaders have taken midcareer turns that have destroyed or interrupted their ministries. Try to find time to read the autobiography of Charles Blair, *The Man Who Could Do No Wrong*, or the biography of Bob Pierce, founder of World Vision, *Days of Glory, Seasons of Night*, written by his daughter, Marilee Pierce Dunker.

What Is the Unpardonable Leadership Sin?

There is considerable controversy in the Bakker/Swaggart aftermath as to whether a known fall from the high standards required of ministers precludes their ever resuming their leadership roles. The question is less whether those two men can be restored than what is the biblical principle involved? Chuck Swindoll, the noted preacher/broadcaster/author, is quite emphatic that a Christian leader's public sin forfeits his right to resuming ministry, even though he seeks God's forgiveness and undertakes a program of rehabilitation under appropriate authority. He certainly is not alone in that position, but other voices disagree, feeling that the redemptive process should be both personal and corporate. My viewpoint on the matter, which differs with Swindoll, is included here for your consideration as your search committee decides whether each candidate must have a blameless record.

Fallen Leaders Are Not "Damaged Goods"

"For over 25 years I have helped businesses find leaders. Recently, I have added Christian organizations to my list of clients. Both groups want good leaders, but I am finding it increasingly difficult to accept the almost universal practice by Christian groups of banishing leaders who have stumbled in their Christian walk.

"It almost seems that forgiveness and love—central themes of our faith—cannot apply to leaders of Christian organizations. We agree that God forgives sinners. We also believe that because God forgives the sinner, we must too. Yet, somehow, Christian organizations rarely find it possible to restore the fallen one to fellowship in a way that eventually allows a return to leadership.

Wrestling with forgiveness

"Could it be that we do not really have a desire to wrestle with implications of genuine forgiveness? Is it easier to interview a new, 'clean' candidate than work with one who can be viewed as tarnished?

"Consider the case of Chuck Colson. His 'sins' and resulting prison term were *before* his spiritual rebirth, so Christians everywhere warmly embraced him with forgiveness. But now that he is one of us, woe to him if he stumbles again. The pattern suggests that he would be stripped of his well-earned leadership role and forever denied a return to it.

"On the other hand, Paul Thayer, former LTV Corporation chief executive officer, recently completed a prison term related to illegal securities trading activities. He has been quickly hired by another firm in a key role because his debt is paid and he is a talented executive. Does the secular world understand forgiveness better than *we* do?

No room for "big" sins

"There are at least two other reasons why Christian leaders seldom get a second chance. Sometimes we shy away from a fallen leader—such as a pastor who has had an affair—because the offense seems so huge. Do we *really* believe in big sins and little sins? To us, adultery may be a big sin; the Bible tells us God views all sin equally. And He offers unlimited grace to cover *any* sin. Such grace will not block the path of restoration for a genuinely repentant fallen leader.

"Selection committees also avoid yesterday's 'fallen' candidates because they worry about public reaction. They fear such a move will lead to the charge of hypocrisy. After all, who wants their pastor preaching against adultery when he, too, was once a victim?

"Yet a fallen and forgiven leader is an effective testimony to the validity of the Christian faith. Such a person eloquently demonstrates that Christians are more identified with redemption than condemnation. The world needs large doses of that message.

"From a practical standpoint, God's people can ill afford to summarily reject leaders who yield to temptation. Not only will we deplete the short supply of current leaders, we will make Christian leadership seem like an impossible career choice. What thoughtful person desires a career where a single moral error could destroy opportunities for future service? Already the glare of public scrutiny is almost too much for pastors, Christian college presidents and leaders of parachurch organizations. We demand optimum moral behavior from these leaders, then reject them permanently when they do not live up to our expectations.

Inoculated by error

"Sometimes I wonder how King David would have fared in a church-related job interview. Before Bathsheba caught his attention, he would have delighted the search committee. But after that tragic fall, the search committee would have clearly labeled him 'damaged goods.'

"Yet I contend that David was a much better candidate *after* Bathsheba, as was Peter after his denials of Christ. The apostle Paul tells us repeatedly of his past errors of persecuting the Church as motivating his service for Christ, though they predate his conversion. Even Moses, the murderer who ran for his life, was later chosen by God to lead His people. People who have experienced the penalties of error have often received an inoculation that gives a future immunity.

"Of course, some use the examples of David and Moses to argue against hiring fallen leaders. They point out that God kept David from building the Temple and Moses from entering the Promised Land. However, they *fail* to mention that despite these penalties, God used these men greatly rather than discarding them.

"God's Word clearly teaches that Christians should join Him in extending to all the reconciliation and restoration that accompany genuine forgiveness. It is what makes our faith so attractive to others.

"Should our leaders be offered less?"[1]

If your search committee shares Swindoll's view, your process is simpler than if you agree with me. Just develop your list of leadership capital offenses and ignore any candidate who—as far as you can determine—has transgressed. You may not find it as simple to build a list of who to keep out as you first imagined. Does doctrinal heresy early in a career count? Or infidelity some years ago? Divorce? Alcoholism? Bankruptcy? You must decide.

If you see a candidate with a blemished past as possibly qualifying for ministry once again, you do not need to develop that potentially troublesome list. Considerably more difficult is the need to try to determine if the repentance and contrition is genuine and if there is an adequate basis for being sure the problem won't arise again. This determination surely will involve the person being willing to submit to authority and to go through an appropriate rehabilitation program that includes a period of time out of the ministry.

If you find such a restored candidate worthy of consideration for your leadership need, you have another formidable challenge yet to face. Can you get your constituency to accept this flawed-and-restored person as their leader? While I believe this action to be scripturally based, it may be no less easy to get it past a congregational vote than mandatory tithing.

When Is It Time for a New Leader?

You know you need a new leader when your previous leader just resigned, retired or died. If the incumbent failed to get a vote of confidence when his performance was reviewed, that's fairly obvious too. Or, if he was just fired for some flagrant sin.

Many times, however, the board and other lay leaders know there is a serious problem in the life of the organization but they are uncertain as to whether it is the leader's fault or if making a change would correct the problem. Here are some indicators to look for:

- *The numbers are slipping:* Membership figures show more people departing than coming in. Income is off. This objective measure is a significant symptom but doesn't reveal the reasons why.
- *Burnout:* Fatigue, irritability and a loss of optimism and enthusiasm on the part of the pastor.
- *Aging or illness:* Lessened energy or available time to devote to ministry. Perhaps a lessened interest in the future of the church.
- *A blurred vision:* The original purpose of the ministry has shifted, the vision blurred, and a new charter or a redefinition is needed to reenergize it.
- *Changed needs:* The life cycle of any organization changes as it matures. Its needs as it is formed can be very different from those of 10-15 years later when a need arises for new leadership skills. Changing from the founder to his successor is usually a traumatic episode.
- *Excessive expectations:* When the expectations of the leader greatly exceed the support of the followers, there is trouble. The reverse is equally true.
- *Political factions:* If the board is opposed to the leader, if the faculty is hostile to the administration, or the congregation is badly split, the adequacy of the leadership needs to be closely examined.

None of these situations automatically call for a new leader, but they all call for corrective action. If the elected leader cannot take the needed steps, perhaps a change is needed. At times, making such a change may not be very fair to the leader because he may not have created the problem. Even so, if the change is required for the organization to survive, and it warrants survival, the change becomes necessary. Great care is needed to recompense the departing leader who was not at fault and to free him from an unwarranted burden of guilt.

A more complex leadership dilemma is encountered where the board, the highest level of authority, is inept or corrupt. Hopefully, the constituency will become aroused and change the board membership or the organization will falter and go out of existence. Corrupt leaders aided by acquiescing boards will, one hopes, meet the same deserved fate.

The Graying of Religious Leadership
Much has been written in recent years about how old our religious leaders are getting and where are their younger replace-

---

Part of the answer to the graying leadership problem is to take some risk with younger, less-proven leaders.

---

ments? The Lausanne Committee has held conferences abroad and in the U.S.A. to identify and encourage young evangelical leaders because of this concern. The perceived shortage may be due to the fact that the very visible leadership that emerged right after World War II has largely retired or died. Some of the concern stems from the aging leaders themselves as they thinly disguise their concern about giving up their own leadership by inquiring, "Who will replace Billy Graham or Ted Engstrom or missionaries like Art Glasser or Sam Moffett?" Others wonder, "When will we hear preaching again like that of Donald Grey Barnhouse or Harold John Ockenga or see another David du Plessis?" Obviously, nostalgia weaves its wonderful spell in Christian circles too.

Part of the answer to the graying leadership problem is to take some risk with younger, less-proven leaders. This gives them a chance to grow into expanded leadership opportunities more quickly, a possibility which is denied them if graying leadership hangs on too long. If careful work is done by the search committee, the selecting of a younger, less-proven leader should not involve too great a risk. Also, younger leaders tend to be more in tune with current problems and ministry methods, rather than tenaciously hanging on to outmoded ones.

> I have had the privilege of assisting 10 Christian parachurch organizations in their searches for new presidents. During a two-month period in early 1988 three of these groups chose young men, 39 to 42 years old, who previously had never run an entire organization. InterVarsity Christian Fellowship chose Dr. Stephen Hayner and LIFE Ministries, which serves in Japan, selected Dr. Stephen Hoke. African Enterprise, a ministry to East and South Africa, made David Montague their new U.S. leader.

These men are outstandingly qualified for these positions except they previously had never been a chief executive. It took courage for the search committees and boards to make such choices.

Is There a Shortage of Ministers?

Yes, and no, depending on who you are. The Presbyterian Church (U.S.A.) has a surplus of candidates, as does the Baptist General Conference, the Reformed Church of America and Missouri Synod Lutherans. Inquiries to the Episcopal Church revealed a shortage of ministers and the Catholic Church has a severe shortage of priests.

Some of the denominations I asked didn't know how many pulpits were open or how many unemployed ministers they had. They don't keep such statistics, they say. Your search committee should do a little research to find out what your situation is before you get started.

A very broad and general answer is that there are numerous possible candidates to look at but most probably are not the answer to your need. However, with prayer, hard work and a good understanding of your group's needs, you will be successful in your search.

My observation about the leadership of parachurch organizations is that there is a drastic shortage of leaders who combine
the communicating skills and the needed managerial abilities.
Christian educational institutions I know less well, but high quality leadership seems to be fairly rare there too. As Yogi Berra
might have said, "The average Christian college president is
rather average."

Finding "God's Man"

Every search committee seeks to find a leader that they feel has
a ministry blessed by God. Some search committees have members with a theological background that leads them to believe
God somehow has preselected a specific perfect man to be their
leader and it is their task to find that person. They believe that if
they somehow miss finding "God's perfect will" for them in this
matter they are sure to have less than the best that God planned
for them.

As you would expect, these people are the same Christians
who believe that God had only one acceptable life partner for
them and only one vocational possibility that God could bless. A
lot of church teaching over the years has fostered the idea of
there being only one choice that pleases God, but is it a scriptural position? If it is, the task of the search committee becomes
so difficult that it scares me.

Dr. Haddon Robinson, president of Denver Seminary, would
say that Scripture is fully adequate to guide a search committee
in finding the type of person that is needed. The principles and
guidelines in the Bible, while adequate, he would say, allow for
the possibility of a number of acceptable candidates, not just
one. He feels God doesn't do the decision-making but tells us
how to do it and trusts us to do so. He even feels that "trying to
find God's will" in making a decision is unscriptural and he dis-
courages the use of "holy hunches" as a basis for decision-
making. Dr. Robinson says, "A hunch is a hunch is a hunch is a
hunch—but God doesn't speak through hunches." Similarly, he
sees circumstances as "factors to be weighed but they are not
signs to be followed" in making decisions.[2]

You may find Dr. Robinson's positions difficult to accept, but I support them and see them as liberating and empowering for a search committee. However, if you agree with him, you do not have a built-in excuse should things not work out with the selection you make. That is, if your committee found "God's man" the only correct choice, it's God's fault if things don't go well. (Come to think of it, could God make a bad choice?) I wonder if people holding such a position are ever conscious of their doing so partially as a way of avoiding having to live with the consequences of the decision?

In 1980, Garry Friesen authored a controversial book that I have found helpful. It is *Decision Making and the Will of God* and I would encourage you to read it, especially if there is disagreement within your committee on this subject. Prof. Friesen seems to see things pretty much as Dr. Robinson does, I might add.

There are a number of books in every seminary library on the subject of knowing the will of God. I have neither the credentials or the temerity to try to instruct you on the subject.

My desire is that you have agreement on your search committee on the way to proceed in your seeking a candidate. If there are any strongly opposing feelings, it is quite important to learn of it as soon as possible and to seek a resolution before candidates are interviewed. Doing so could take some time, thought and prayer. The committee can function on either basis (only one acceptable candidate vs. several) but the divided committee will have a major impediment in completing the search successfully.

Notes
1. Robert W. Dingman, "Fallen Leaders Are Not 'Damaged Goods,'" *Christianity Today*, December 10, 1987, p. 12. Used by permission.
2. Haddon Robinson, in a series of Businessmen's Breakfast Bible Studies, Denver, Colorado, during the early 1980s. Used by permission.

CHAPTER TWO
SUSTAINING THE LEADERLESS FLOCK

THE task of the church search committee is greatly impacted by the attitude of the congregation about the departing pastor. If the membership gave a collective sigh of relief as he left, it is a very different situation than if he had been dearly loved. When a departure leaves opposing factions still feuding and the scars from recent wounds are still an angry red, it's an even more difficult situation. A sensitive search committee will assess the emotional residue from the prior pastor's leadership and plan accordingly to meet the needs of the congregation. The same is true of the Christian educational institution or parachurch ministry, though perhaps to a lesser degree.

Replacing a Founder/Leader
The need for this sensitivity is greatest when the search is being done to replace the founder of a church or parachurch ministry. All of the members and staff have joined the group during the founder's leadership and only his vision and guiding hand has led

these people. It is understandable that the emotional potential of making the change is high.

Organizational consultants will tell you that the change from a founder—who often acts like an owner—is a crisis moment in the life of any organization. As you form the search committee, do all you can to keep it free from the influence of the founder. His vision for the ministry may now be out of date.

Achieving Closure

Before the search committee can get their constituency ready to consider a new leader, it is necessary to have good closure on the ministry of the departing leader.

> We were the deacon board, the group directing the spiritual life of our non-denominational church, and we were together in a member's nice mountain cabin near Lake Arrowhead. It was an annual affair devoted to getting to know each other better and praying and planning with the pastor for the next year. Our highly respected pastor, Dr. Robert Schaper, dropped the bomb on us early in the weekend by saying he was leaving to join the faculty and administration of a nearby seminary. We were surprised, hurt and even angry. How dare he interrupt the blessing we felt God was giving us! I was still smarting as we drove down the mountain, but the feeling was perceptibly moving into a sense of loss and even sadness. What would become of us without Bob? As our grousing diminished and our fog of uncertainty dissipated, we began a period of concentrated prayer. That was quickly followed by a growing sense of reluctant excitement as we looked to the future and selected a search committee to find our next pastor.

It was more than 20 years later when I became a hospice volunteer counseling the terminally ill that I learned that we had done exactly what Dr. Elizabeth Kubler-Ross says everyone does when suffering the loss of a loved one. Denial, anger, bar-

"The worst case of pastor burnout I've ever seen."

Source: *Leadership,* Spring 1988, p. 67. Reprinted by permission of Lee Johnson.

gaining, depression and then acceptance are the classic stages she describes, and we went through each one as if she was there coaching us.

The literature concerning how individuals and groups handle a sense of loss is helpful to a search committee which seeks to understand the mourning of a congregation or staff while getting on with the business of preparing them for a growth experience

---

Saying farewell to your leader is more than a courtesy; it is a necessary ritual.

---

that can emerge from this somber period. If you recently fired your leader and have a great sense of relief at his going, none of this applies to you, of course.

Saying Good-bye

Saying farewell to your leader is more than a courtesy; it is a necessary ritual. The administration of the college or the congregation of a church will not be fully ready to welcome a new leader until they have concluded the relationship with their prior leader. Ideally, the person who is leaving is best situated to make the closure happen.

Roy Oswald, who studies pastor/congregation relationships, says about pastors who are leaving, "Usually they slip off into the night without really saying good-bye, and that can undercut everything they've done up till then. People may question whether the pastor really cared for them at all."[1]

Oswald feels saying good-bye is more than just a big farewell party. "Closure takes a minimum of two or three months. In one sense, you are a lame duck, but that's good. You can stop programming and bolstering your favorite activities.

"Your task now is closure, and that takes time, especially if you're well liked. People's initial reaction is shock and denial. They can't say good-bye on the spot. There's a subtle withdrawal, and then they come back. Good closure prevents lots of problems. Pastors don't realize that in order to start well in a new parish, they must say good-bye to the old parish."[2]

The Interregnum

Interregnum a Latin term meaning "between the reigns" and referring to that period existing between kings, if one king hadn't killed his predecessor and occupied the throne before it got cold. While intrigue and power plays are not unknown in Christian circles, succession happily doesn't take that form.

If you are a leader retiring, that fact usually is known well in advance and a replacement found in a timely fashion so no vacancy ever develops. That is the ideal situation—no discontinuity in leadership.

Rev. Joseph Stowell became president of Moody Bible Institute in 1987, following the retirement of Dr. George Sweeting. The search committee started their work far enough in advance to allow a two and one-half month period for Stowell to be on board as president-elect before he had to shoulder any responsibilities. Moody is a large, complex organization and the newly installed President Stowell told me how much he appreciated the opportunity to learn the organization before he had to make any decisions. He knows the importance of not making mistakes with key personnel or in organizational changes during the initial months of a new administration.[3]

While no *interregnum* at all is the best of all worlds, it doesn't normally work out that way. Usually it can't because someone has convinced your present leader that he is needed as soon as possible in the new situation. The patience of the new group seldom exceeds three months and the search to replace him almost never can be done in that time. If your departing president or pastor gives you a three-month notice, you may face a six-to-twelve-month gap in leadership. In such a case, the challenge of the *interregnum* is yours, like it or not.

If you are chairman of the search committee, I hope you are not also chairman of the board that runs your organization. It is a very heavy load to bear. If you must do both for some reason, arrange so that, for a 6-12 month period, your family will get along without seeing a lot of you and shift your duties on your regular job to associates as much as you can.

"Change is opportunity, not a threat," says Dr. Peter F. Drucker.[4] Viewed from a top management perspective, I'm sure he is correct, but I doubt that subordinates feel that way. Neither do most of the people sitting in the pew Sunday after Sunday. If they became members during the ministry of the departing pastor, they may be especially prone to anxiety about what is going on.

The challenge of managing the *interregnum* is to reassure the anxious, to convince the worshipers that God is still at work among you and that things are moving in the right direction. The search committee needs to coordinate closely with those leading the organization to assure that the new leader will not come to an anemic, dispirited group of people.

There are a number of ways to get across that positive message during this difficult transition time.

Keep them informed
Physicists say that nature abhors a vacuum. So do anxious groups who can't learn what's going on. Change gives rise to rumors and such rumors seem to get distorted to fit the anxieties of the situation. A good search committee will give their constituency regular reports that progress is being made. While you can't say who you are talking to, activity reports can be made. Bellevue Presbyterian, in Washington state, even used graphic displays in the church foyer to inform worshipers during their last search. That's creative. See what you can come up with.

Schedule special events
Show that the vitality of your church didn't leave with your former pastor. This is a great time for inviting "name" preachers, gifted teachers, special music talent and seminar leaders to minister to various parts of the congregation. If you can energize your choir to a higher performance level, that in itself provides a weekly reminder that the church is healthy and God did not leave with the departed pastor.

Reassure the staff
From the church secretary, the custodian and the junior pastoral

staff, the congregation gets subtle messages that can shape their expectations. If the church staff feels threatened and insecure, they can have a damaging effect on morale generally.

Hopefully, your church does not follow the rule that all the church staff must submit their resignation so that the new leader can choose whomever he wants. Even if your church does, wisely offer assurances to the staff that adequate provision will be made for them to make a good transition if they do not choose to work under the new senior pastor. The *interregnum* needs extra effort from all the staff and that commitment is not possible if they are primarily doing their own job search during this period.

The Interim Pastor

A church cannot function with an empty pulpit, so prompt steps must be taken to fill it. Should the search committee handle this task or the church board? Either could handle it well, but close coordination is needed if it is split.

If your departing pastor was your only ordained minister, you may quickly need to seek out an interim pastor. As you face up to a year with an empty pulpit, you must have someone who can marry, bury and offer the sacraments. However, if you have other ordained staff, this pressure does not exist. That capability allows you the freedom to seek out any of a variety of guest preachers, teachers, missionaries or evangelists. You could never do this on a series of Sundays when your pastor was with you, but now is your opportunity.

Where do you find interim pastors? Try your denominational sources. Or, if you are an independent church, ask around. You should be able to find several other churches who have used interim pastors during a transitional period. Who did they use and with what results?

When you find someone, I suggest you have him preach several times before you offer a more ex•ended employment arrangement. You do not want an unacceptable preacher causing people to drop out.

Interim pastors are often retired or semiretired ministers who are available for short-term assignments. A few denominations have full-time ministers available who are not retired but have specialized in this form of ministry.

Check out your prospective interim pastor carefully. If your church is full of hurt people after a bruising separation from your former pastor, you may wish to find an interim who can help bring healing. An aggressive ex-evangelist or a learned, though dry, seminary professor would not be ideal choices for this situation. Sense what your needs are right now and see if you can find an interim who can best prepare the congregation for your new pastor.

It is important that your interim pastor not have aspirations for your pulpit, so be clear about that prohibition when he is employed. His role is to maintain the life of the church during this period of transition and to do all he can to prepare the congregation for new leadership.

Forgetting the Past

Paul tells us in Philippians 3:13 that he laid aside past things so that he could focus his attention and efforts on pressing forward to what is ahead. He then encourages us to do so too as part of our spiritual maturing.

A creative search committee working with a sensitive interim pastor can assist a whole congregation in this process. Here is an example:

> Our departing pastor was an eloquent preacher and highly esteemed by everyone for this skill. His rich imagery, his clarity of thinking, his avoidance of trite phrases and cliches—all those things made him tough to replace. Our search committee decided to deliberately keep the pulpit open for a year and to have a number of speakers be with us during this year. We hoped that this would make it easier for the new pastor because the congregation would have at least partially forgotten the preaching excellence we had known and which we did not expect to match again.

As you select the interim pastor, seek out someone who does not remind the congregation of your recently departed pastor. A different age, a dissimilar appearance and an unfamiliar preaching style would be good ways to reduce the remembrances of the former leader.

If the termination of the earlier relationship was unpleasant, the memories are probably unpleasant too. But if the now-absent leader was greatly loved and is sorely missed, remembering him can create a sense of loss and emptiness. If possible, try to avoid them both. As Paul wisely counseled the believers of his day, "Forgetting what is behind . . . . press on" (Phil. 3:13-14, *NIV*).

Defining the Interim's Role

Some care is needed to spell out to your fill-in pastor what it is you expect him to do. Enumerate for him what it is you expect and how many hours you expect it to take each week. Is it to be full-time or part-time?

You may wish to have your interim pastor preach only three weeks a month while continuing to perform pastoral duties throughout the month. This allows you to have the benefits of continuity while having special-emphasis speakers to enliven the church program. The compensation arrangements should reflect your agreement.

Will you want an open-ended arrangement so that either party can end it with two or four weeks' notice? Or, should it be for a solid six months? If so, what conditions could lead to that term being changed? When this interim pastor does not live locally, what are the arrangements for housing expenses and transportation?

Whatever arrangements you make, the congregation also needs to know what to expect of the interim pastor. If a youth group wants him to teach a class on Sundays and the women's missionary group desires him as a speaker, he is likely to get into trouble if he is only being paid to preach on Sunday.

Mobilizing the Lay Leadership

When you are between leaders, everyone has to work harder to take up the slack. Some of the best church lay leadership will be so busy on the search committee that they cannot serve in their usual roles as committee people, teachers or board members. With your lay leadership resources thus weakened, you need to find new people or recycle experienced ones to fill in the gaps.

Special recruiting and training efforts may be needed and appeals can be made for them to serve, as we were told in World War II, "for the duration." In this case, the duration is that of the search process. This increased pressure during the transitional period can be appealing to some members, who now feel really needed. On the other hand, if your departed leader developed a primarily personal following, the paddle will seem small and the paddlers few as you try to gather speed from way, way up the creek.

A Valuable Resource
I would encourage you to read the fine booklet, *The Interim Pastor,* published by the Alban Institute of Washington, D.C.

The Acting President
For the college, seminary or parachurch group, the "interim" idea is difficult to implement. Usually some key manager is appointed acting president or acting executive director while the search is undertaken. Hopefully, there are competent people in the organization who can hold things together. If not, a committee from the board may act as a president would. In 1987, Inter-Varsity Christian Fellowship met their need for interim leadership by appointing a board member, Tom Dunkerton, a recently retired business executive, to act in an interim capacity. He served with distinction.

An outsider should be brought in to be an acting CEO under only unusual circumstances. During the 1986-87 academic year at North Park College, they had an organizational and financial crisis. They brought in Dr. Pat LaTorre, a consensus builder and a good administrator. His skills set the stage well for the selection of Dr. David Horner, whose administration got off to a great start.

The more conventional approach is what Whitworth College did when Dr. Bob Mounce retired. Joe Black, the vice president of Development, was made acting president and served until Dr.

Arthur DeJong was selected through the efforts of the search committee. Joe then moved back into his development role.

In each instance, a change in leadership had been successfully accomplished and the *interregnum* between leaders had proved to be a time of growth, maturation and a new focus for the institutions concerned.

Notes
1. Roy Oswald, "The Pastor's Passages," *Leadership,* Fall 1983. Used by permission.
2. Ibid.
3. Information used by permission of the Reverend Joseph Stowell.
4. "Drucker on Change" in "Musings of the Sage," *Reflections from the Lamp* 3 (Winter 1987): 2.

CHAPTER THREE

FORMING THE SEARCH COMMITTEE

W HEN the search committee is formed, half the damage is already done! That statement of mine may sound somewhat cynical, but it points out a truth that repeatedly asserts itself in search committees I have seen or heard about: Too often the leadership of an organization responds too quickly to the news of a need for a new leader.

To create a search committee that is full of promise and has a high probability of success requires some thought and planning. No event is likely to be as crucial to the next 10 years of your church, college or parachurch group as the shaping of this committee, so it warrants the best thinking possible—and that kind of thinking seldom comes in an instant.

How to Get Started
Your organization's top elected person may be a board president, chairman of the deacons or trustees or some other title. If you are organized as Presbyterians are, your departing pastor was moderator of the Session, and you now have no leader to assist

in shaping the needed Pastor Nominating Committee, as they
call it. A call to the Presbytery Committee should provide you
with an advisor who will tell you how to get things rolling. If you
are a congregation in Church of the Nazarene, a call to the district superintendent can result in your having more done for you
than you may even wish, if you want to shape your own future.

Whoever your leader is, he needs to decide how best to set
up the search committee and do all he can to insure its success.
Reading this book is a helpful preparatory step in getting all
available material from any denominational sources you have.
My inquiries revealed the Baptist General Conference and the
Cumberland Presbyterians as having some of the best-
developed materials to assist search committees. Surprisingly,
some large denominations offer very little to assist the churches
they serve.

Your leader faces questions such as these:
- Who should chair the search committee?
- Who will serve well under that person's leadership?
- Should I be a member of the committee too, or can I serve
  best by staying at a distance from it?
- If the organization's best leaders are already busy with
  other responsibilities, will appointing them to this demand-
  ing task cripple other vital activities?
- What special interest groups need representation on the
  committee?
- Should the selection criteria be developed by our board or
  by the search committee and approved by us?
- How well will our group function until we have a new leader,
  and how long will that be?
- Will our income drop without a leader and how much will a
  search effort cost?

In the business world, the executive making these questions
is well compensated for making good decisions, but in Christian
circles this person is usually a volunteer working for the love of
the organization and the ministry.

APPOINT OR ELECT?
If there is a competent leader or committee in charge of things,

"In the minutes, should I record this as a
'vigorous theological discussion' or a 'serious
ecclesiastical debate'?"

Source: *Leadership*, Summer 1987, p. 33. Reprinted by permission of John V. Lawing, Jr.

the appointing of search committee members is the preferred
way. Fewer things can go wrong with well-chosen, appointed
members. If a congregation is asked to elect search committee
members, the danger is in the congregation not knowing what is
needed to serve well or who will have the needed commitment.

In the college setting, there is some danger that, if the faculty and student body have the opportunity to choose their own
committee representatives, they may elect people who are so
partisan and parochial in their views that they harm the unity of
the committee. If the political consequences are manageable,
the appointing of members is the preferred method.

When an organization has a highly charged political environment, particularly a church, an election of committee members
may be a necessary alternative but appointments can still work if
there is careful balancing of the factions. A parallel situation
would be a congressional committee where the Republicans and
Democrats are appointed in equal numbers, but the chairperson
should in this case be an "independent" so that efforts do not
become deadlocked.

Whether members are selected by appointment or election,
it is essential that the search committee has the confidence of
the church or board, so that when candidates are presented
there is a proclivity to accept the recommendation, not reject it.

The Chairperson
The qualities the chairperson needs
Selecting the wrong chairperson is the best way I know of to
impair the proper functioning of a search committee. This person should have the respect of associates and a personality
strong enough not to be dominated by others yet not so strong
as to suffocate the thoughts of committee members. A high
energy level is needed plus the quality of persistence required to
"hang in there" for a year or more, if the search drags on. An
indecisive person should not be considered for even committee
membership, because the basic function is to make a series of
tough decisions.

When you consider someone to be chairperson, try to find
someone who has ample time to do the job and free him from all

other responsibilities. Try to avoid anyone who just took a new job, has heavy family commitments, travels a lot in his work or whose spouse will resent the heavy time demands involved. A retired person could be a good choice in terms of available time.

Skills the chairperson needs

- Has the ability to organize the overall tasks and separate out tasks for the various subcommittees;
- Delegates well and gets the needed results on a timely basis;
- Can mediate differences of opinion and obtain consensus;
- Has the ability to develop a cohesive team with a high level of commitment;
- Is a good communicator who can deal effectively with committee members, candidates, the board, any needed denominational contacts, the board members, employees or students of the organization and the related constituencies. Colleges have alumni interests to consider and all groups have donors to consider.

Usually, this needed experience can most easily be found among those who have done an outstanding job of chairing a church or board committee of importance. If the organization has been politically polarized, the chairperson should ideally be as neutral as possible. Choosing a chairperson from a faction can be interpreted as "stacking the deck" and can create an acceptance problem for the person selected.

The Committee Members
The composition of the committee

A search committee should seek certain skills as it recruits members, but those skills must be in persons who will also have cooperative spirits. Also, in a pastoral search, determination must be made whether representation on the committee should be given to the youth ministry, Christian education, the seniors, missions and other aspects of ministry. You are fortunate, if fully qualified members are available from each area, but don't load your committee with deadheads in the name of "total representation." You can get the input of the youth ministry, for example, and let them know their concerns are being fully considered without getting an inexperienced 18-year-old involved as a committee member.

The expertise of the committee
Previously, we discussed the skills the chairperson needs. But individual members also should bring to the committee specific fields of expertise or knowledge, if these are available to you:

- A person with management know-how;
- Someone who is theologically astute;
- A party with interviewing and assessment skills;
- A writer;
- Someone with a feel for financial matters;
- A person with good logical and analytical abilities, perhaps a lawyer;
- Hopefully, a number of deeply spiritual people;
- Someone who knows the background of the organization and any denominational ties it may have.

Some time ago I might have suggested including someone who travels a lot in his work so he can "listen" for the committee at churches where the candidates might be. However, these days many pastors, mission executives and college presidents have audiotapes of their presentations so that less initial travel is needed.

Personal qualities of committee members
Your list may be better than mine, but let me state what I would seek as qualities *each* member should have, if possible.

- Eager to serve; not coerced into it;
- Has the available time;
- Strong enough to speak up but not a dominating personality who will inhibit others;
- Has a positive, can-do attitude and a good energy level;

- Is a fairly intelligent person with an education representative of the congregation;
- Has previously been an effective committee member;
- Can maintain confidences (even from their spouse), and
- Is a decisive person.

The processes that a search committee goes through all lead to making a final decision about a candidate. On the way to that final one, many earlier decisions must be made as other candidates are dismissed. While some decisions are simple to make and are almost black-and-white, many are less clear and quite difficult. In some cases you will find your heart leaning one way and your mind in an opposing one, and to the latter you must take heed.

As the search committee is formed, it is *essential* that the people who are to serve not have great problems in making decisions. If you know fairly well the people who are being considered, you should be able to avoid individuals who tend to agonize over life's decisions. Such a person would be an impediment to the committee and would be emotionally distressed by the duties to be performed.

The Time Required
The search process is unlikely to be shorter than four or five months and can take up to a year or more for a college or a congregation. The time needed varies, depending on how quickly you want the task done and how well you provide the needed resources.

So You're on the Search Committee[1] quotes two examples of the time required of a committee member doing a pastoral search. One met 11 times for a total of 45 hours over a six-month period. The other met 29 times for 54 hours over an 18-month span. Remember, my friend, that those figures are only for the hours spent in committee meetings. Many of the search tasks are not done in meetings, such as handling correspondence, filling out forms, checking references, making phone contacts, undertaking travel and so on.

Here is how the chairman of the Whitworth College presidential search committee reported to the board in 1987. "Of the 258 names referred to us, 158 persons became formal applicants for the position. As a committee over the last 17 months, we had 26 meetings for a total of 279 hours as a committee of the whole. In addition, various subcommittees spent many more hours screening and traveling to interview candidates. And that doesn't count hours reading dossiers, processing information or telephoning up to 15 to 20 references on some candidates. By one committee member's estimate, we made 1800 phone calls." This statement shows how massive an effort the search process can become, but in most instances it will not grow to this size.

As you can see, this committee assignment can be more intensive than any normal one. If your church board meets monthly for three hours and you also chair a committee reporting to it that takes two hours a month, that's 60 hours a year. I predict a normal search committee will consume more than that much time. To avoid burnout, the organization should try to free the search committee members from other duties. I realize this action can strip other leadership roles of needed people, but no task is more important than finding the new leader.

How Large?
That depends. The search committee should be large enough to avoid wearing anyone out, yet as small as that will permit, plus one. Smaller committees can work more effectively, if the needed skills and horsepower are there. The "plus one" is because someone will probably drop out along the way for some reason. Also, I prefer an odd number of members so there will never be a tie vote.

Five or seven members makes the individual load very heavy. Nine, eleven or thirteen seems better for the congregation or college, but that's too big for the board of a parachurch organization. Typically, this last group gets some administrative support and that eases the load.

The Committee's Charter
More search committees than I care to remember get in trouble because somewhere along the line they become unsure of what

they have been told to do. The charter should be written out and understood by the board and the committee. Typically, this is done by motions that are put in the minutes.

The basic starting point for the search committee is the mission statement of the organization. It defines the purpose and nature of the group and serves as the map for the search committee as they seek the new leader who can move the organization to meet those objectives. If no mission statement exists, if it is out of date or is pretty fuzzy in what it says, the search committee should require a new one before moving ahead. That vision of the future is the bedrock on which the search committee builds.

The charter should also include:

- Composition of the selection committee, including any needed replacements.
- Clarification on whether the board needs to approve the selection criteria and compensation package; and,
- The budget established for the search;
- A target date for completion;
- Progress-reporting requirements;
- Stipulations as to what minutes are to be kept;
- Guidance on whether one candidate is to be presented to the board, or more;
- Authorization, if the committee is to negotiate the compensation package;
- Specifics on how the selection procedure works, such as recommendation to the board for approval, denominational approval required, and so on.

Very few boards know enough to provide this needed guidance to the search committee. Whatever they fail to mention or could not know in advance, the chair of the committee should prepare as a recommendation to the board and obtain their approval before moving on with the search.

The Costs of a Search

What should be budgeted for a search effort? It depends on the scope of your search. A locally focused search—within a hundred miles—can be done with very little expense.

The 1988 search of InterVarsity Christian Fellowship for a new president was of national scope and required search committee members to come together from all around the country and candidates being considered from great distances too. A college presidency search involves a large committee and much travel. Search costs can exceed $30,000 to $40,000 in such cases.

As you plan your search, you must shape your budget to fit your plan. Here are the major items to plan for:

- Secretarial help
- Postage and printing
- Telephone expense—lots of it
- Travel of committee members
- Travel of candidates, including hotel or temporary housing
- Relocation costs for the family of the candidate

For the time you have a vacancy in your leadership position you have a saving in that salary, but for a church that saving is diminished by the cost of those who fill the pulpit.

It is obvious that the financial cost of a search can be substantial. Even so, it is prudent to spend whatever is needed to do a thorough search because, if it is done badly, the results can be disastrous. A poor choice of a leader usually takes a year or two to become so evident that remedial action is taken. The new search effort is undermined by a spirit of a recent failure and a reluctance of those who served on the first search committee to serve again. (Nor does anyone want them to serve again.) The emotional toll and organizational disarray resulting from a second search effort is enormous. The very possibility of it should serve to motivate any search committee to do their task so well that it will never be necessary to repeat it.

The Risks and Rewards of Serving on the Search Committee

There are good reasons why a Christian who is asked to serve on a search committee should accept. An awareness of these reasons is useful in persuading those who are being approached to serve:

The rewards

First, it is an opportunity for significant ministry for God and with a group you belong to and believe in. The search process will shape the future of the organization for some time to come and is a pivotal action in its life. You can have a key role in what will happen.

Do not expect much recognition from your church or the board of the group for your work. But if your motives for serving are correct, this lack of recognition won't bother you.

Second, it is an opportunity for personal growth. You will learn more about your organization than you ever knew before. Also, you will learn about the motivations and frustrations of the type of leaders you are searching for. Your assessment and evaluation skills will be sharpened.

Third, you may well find that your frustrations with the search process drives you to a deeper dependence on God and a more vital prayer life as you seek His guidance. You will probably reshape your ideas about how to know God's leading in making key decisions.

Fourth, you will very likely develop a deep respect and caring for your fellow committee members from your labors together.

Do *not* expect much recognition from your church or the board of the group for your work. It just doesn't seem to happen that way. But if your motives for serving are correct, this lack of recognition won't bother you.

Another reason to serve warrants mention, and whether it is noble or ignoble varies with your viewpoint. You may decide to serve as a way of making a needed change in the direction of the organization. Or, to stop a change from happening that you strongly oppose. This, too, can be a valid reward for serving and it has a risk in it as well, in case you lose out.

The risks

If I mention the potential rewards, I am compelled to mention the negative aspects, too.

First, probably the worst risk is that you choose the wrong leader, the organization is badly damaged, and the search committee is viewed as having done a lousy job.

Second, you pay a price in the rearranging of your work life and your personal life to take on this major assignment. Unaccustomed time pressures may build that can impact on your job and family. Your spouse may resent your inability to share with her/him the details of committee activities.

Third, the chance to admire and respect your fellow committee members may not work out that way. People who are difficult, dumb or intransigent won't change just because they go on a search committee. If the environment before the search was hostile and acrimonious, it may continue that way. Also, if you have Christian leaders and pastors comfortably on a pedestal in your mind, you may well be distressed to find out about their humanity and weaknesses. But it will be good for you in the long run.

The most compelling reason to serve on the search committee is that someone has to do it and, if you are seen as qualified, why shouldn't it be you?

The Confidentiality Commitment

Time and time again, I will bring up the need for all committee members to honor scrupulously a promise not to reveal any of the identities of candidates or the details that are learned about their backgrounds. Great damage can be done to individuals, their families and their present places of ministry by misuse or premature disclosure of ongoing discussions. To do this would be an act unworthy of your organization and of you and your Christian calling.

The commitment to confidentiality should be to each other by committee members because, if one indiscretion results in an injury, the whole committee falls into some disrepute. To any candidate who is not unemployed or has not declared his intent to leave, a promise of confidentiality is offered. To references providing information on candidates, still another promise of secrecy is extended. At all levels, this promise needs to operate. You are playing with people's careers and reputations in the search process—and this responsibility should always be in your awareness.

I recommend that as references are checked on candidates of interest to you, you avoid sharing "juicy items" that may be uncovered. The person obtaining the disqualifying data can share it privately with the committee chairperson without an open discussion. Why tempt a committee member with information they do not need to know?

All my life has been spent in Christian churches and colleges or other church-related groups and, in my opinion, gossip flies faster in Christian circles than in secular ones. Our high standards make any departure from them a matter of greater interest than elsewhere. The relative rarity of scandalous or compromising information adds to the intensity of interest, and the stories fly swiftly. Unhappily, negative items seem to be used with the same avidness as in non-Christian circles, but the wounding power is much greater where love, caring and rectitude are the norm.

The mechanics of maintaining confidentiality requires a little thought:

- Should mail be marked "Personal & Confidential"? Perhaps it should be sent to the committee member's office, not home.
- Where will files be kept and who will be doing the typing and distributing the copies?
- Should candidates be called at their homes or their offices?
- What should be said if a candidate's secretary asks the purpose of the call?
- When you visit a candidate's church to hear a sermon, what is the response to the friendly member who asks, "What brings you to be with us today?"

Sloppy precautions for maintaining confidentiality can accidentally create a problem for a candidate that is no less real than an intentional one. A high probability is that "pillow talk" will be the greatest source of leaks. Having extracted a promise of secrecy from the spouse, a committee member shares a piece of confidential information. In this way, the member has let slip out information intended for his ears only, and has done so only because of a failure to see how important confidentiality is to the integrity of the committee's function.

As a candidate is dropped from consideration, why not dispose of his file as soon as possible? Especially, if negative data is in it. When the search is completed, a good practice is to dispose of all files.

I confess that I would encourage you to save the file of "the other candidate," if there was a strong second one and you hold some misgivings about how things will turn out with the person you selected. We hope this is not a situation you will face.

Ethics for a Search Committee

Why should the question of ethics arise? Shouldn't a pervasive Christian spirit on the part of everyone concerned preclude such an issue? Theoretically, yes, but not necessarily. When we go into unfamiliar areas we can unintentionally get into trouble.

Careful attention is required throughout the selection process to assure that fair treatment is accorded everyone involved in the effort. The ethical challenges can be looked at from the viewpoints of the various people or groups involved.

Search committee member concerns

- Good ethics require you to place the needs of the congregation and the efforts of the committee above your own viewpoint and pet ideas;
- Both ethical and practical reasons require that, as a committee member, you assume your share of the tasks to be done and that you do them on schedule;
- As a representative of the congregation or parachurch organization, you are ethically required to speak up and to be an

active participant and doing so prohibits you from being dominated by a stronger personality or power block on the committee.

Responsibilities to other Christian organizations or churches

- Sensitivity to the needs of the Church as a whole requires that meeting the leadership needs of your organization not be your sole concern. You must consider what will happen to your candidate's present place of ministry if you enlist him to serve with you.

Obligations to candidates

- *Absolute* confidential handling of all candidate information is an ethical necessity. If a committee member has the compulsion to share everything with his or her spouse, that person should not be on the committee.
- Integrity obligates the committee to be as open with a candidate concerning the negatives of the job and the congregation/organization as with the positive factors.
- Discretion, wisdom and Christian concern dictate that no action should be taken which might injure the present ministry of a prospective candidate.
- Courtesy and Christian love mandate that every candidate be handled with caring concern and sensitivity. If that is done consistently, the contact with your search committee will result in candidates never feeling "used" or demeaned by the experience. Bringing about such positive results requires a timely and kindly response to every candidate you have contacted.

Treatment of the new leader

- In negotiating compensation with the incoming leader, care should be taken not to exploit any lack of financial sophistication. If the new leader later realizes that he has been

taken advantage of, a distrust develops that can sour a promising relationship.
- Any committee member who voted against the new leader's selection should *never* let that be known outside the committee. The new leader deserves the support of everyone if he is called to minister.

Search committee members have responsibilities to the organization they serve, to the other members, to the Christian community, to the candidates, to themselves and to the Christ we serve. I can think of no better guidance to cover all these concerns than this:

Love is patient, love is kind. It does not envy, it does not boast, it is not proud. It is not rude, it is not self-seeking, it is not easily angered, it keeps no record of wrongs. Love does not delight in evil but rejoices with the truth. It always protects, always trusts, always hopes, always perseveres (1 Cor. 13:4-7, *NIV*).

Does Prayer Help?

What a heretical question for Christians! Of course, it does! However, you and I can think of situations where strong Christians were on a search committee and surrounded their efforts by prayer, yet they made a terrible selection. How can that be, if prayer really works and God cares what happens to His people.

Review your own thinking on the subject of prayer and see how your ideas fit the tasks of a search committee. I am no theologian, so I suspect I'm on dangerous ground here, but let me also suggest a few thoughts on prayer for us to consider together.

If a praying search committee selects the wrong person who then has to be replaced later, does that mean God didn't hear their prayers or care about the outcome of their search? I believe He hears and does care but not in a way that causes Him to force a correct decision on every praying search committee. After all, whether this choice is poor or inspired, God is certain of His own ultimate victory. It's not His reputation that's at stake, is it?

If God supernaturally inspired all praying search committees so that all made "perfect" selections, He would, I believe, have to invade our personalities in a way that would change the nature of free will. Nevertheless, in both biblical and contemporary times are occasions when God seems to have done such an extraordinary thing. Keeping that thought in mind, I think we should always ask God for His leading even while we work as hard as if we believe He won't answer us.

A bozo who has been blessed by a praying search committee is still a bozo. Prayer is essential, but prayer alone is not all that is needed.

If we believe in a direct cause-and-effect between prayer, the subsequent actions of the search committee and the one who is selected, God has a lot to answer for. I have seen search committees with great prayer warriors who also had members full of personal pride, bigotry and animosity to other members. Some committee members are lazy and others try to subvert the search process while still others are untruthful or try to push a friend or relative into the open position.

Can God bless such efforts? Should He be blamed for the poor results because various "churchy" things were done? No way!

Praying search committees that won't work hard or learn how to do their job well are not God's fault, even when their failures reflect negatively on their Christian groups. Such committees should be expected to select bozos. Remember, a bozo who has been blessed by a praying search committee is still a bozo. Prayer is essential, but prayer alone is not all that is needed.

The perceptible benefit that a praying search committee enjoys is that as they pray for each other, they are more likely to be building the needed trust and basis for cooperation that a good committee requires. As I have, you probably have served with groups where the opposing views of members impeded progress until praying together caused the differences to melt away. When we genuinely seek God's guidance in prayer it tends to moderate our intransigence while opening us up to a more broadened understanding and basis for cooperation.

Similarly, a congregation upholding the search committee in prayer builds a supportive attitude and expectancy that is essential in meeting the needs of a congregation, college or parachurch organization. If I'm correct, such intercessory prayer is both needed and valid, yet not a perfect guarantee that the search committee will do all that it can and should do.

The Form of Prayer Support

My personal preference concerning prayer support is that a group meet regularly, probably weekly, for the primary purpose of supporting the search committee's efforts for as long as the search takes. Meetings of the search committee should open with a thoughtful devotional and prayer should both precede and conclude the meetings. An appropriate prayer that ends a bruising committee meeting can go a long way toward restoring a spirit of cooperation.

Throughout the entire search process, each group in the church should make the search a matter of continuing prayer. To that end, each Sunday School class, committee meetings—everybody, will be praying about the leader that is being sought. Similarly, in the Christian college or Bible school setting, students, faculty, board members and administrators will ask God to guide the search process through the efforts of the committee members.

You are undoubtedly the best one to shape the prayer support system for your organization. You know what would be comfortable and supportable within your group. For instance, you may wish to make this particular prayer effort rather special in the way you set things up, so that intercession for the search process is not just one more item for prayer.

After all, what is more important for all concerned than finding the next leader? Be careful, however, not to make the prayer effort so ambitious that it cannot be sustained for a year or more, if the search should take that long.

Note
1. Bunty Ketcham, *So You're on the Search Committee* (Washington, D.C.: Alban Institute, Inc., 1985), 24 pp. The Alban Institute is located at 4125 Nebraska Avenue, NW, Washington, DC 20016.

CHAPTER FOUR

WHO ARE WE? WHERE ARE WE GOING?

IF you have been active in the leadership of your church or college for five or more years you probably feel you know your group pretty well. Many boards change their composition slowly, allowing three successive three-year terms. If the leadership is effective, this continuity is highly desirable. Even so, such an arrangement creates the possibility of an entrenched group becoming complacent and getting out of touch with the needs of the organization.

Most organizations do not have occasion to do a search for a new leader more often than at five- to ten-year intervals. Given the lapse of that much time, whatever the perceptions were of what the organization was before, the situation is sure to be different now. To spell out all the factors involved—whether obvious or subtle—is not necessary to confirm that changes have taken place since the last leader was selected.

Even if the organization has been held in suspended animation with no change taking place, getting the participation of the organizational "family" in the selection process is still important.

After all, they will be making the final choice as they affirm the work of the search committee, so ensuring their involvement as early as possible is essential. We all tend to feel that a decision is of better quality if we have had a hand in making it. Also, if we have had input that helped shape the decision, we are more likely to support it in the future.

Who Are We?

Who are we? is a question that can be answered partially by demographic data. A congregation with 60 percent of its members over age 45, 75 percent college graduates and a median income of over $35,000 has little in common with another church that is younger, less educated and earning less.

Looking at your group in the broader context of the community it serves is a meaningful way to know who your group is. For instance, a high percentage of older members is to be expected in retirement areas such as in certain parts of Florida or Arizona. But in average communities a similar percentage of seniors may mean that the church has been ineffective in its youth programs.

Similarly, declining membership and income will mean one thing in a church caught in the depressed economic conditions of towns dominated by the hurting industries of steel, lumbering or mining, or in one caught in a decaying inner city. The same data may have a very different meaning in a suburban church near a major city.

The economic data for your research of the surrounding area is available from governmental sources, chambers of commerce and other public and business sources. The internal data concerning your constituency is obtained by querying them directly. If you are fortunate enough to be with a group who has a self-study or has written a long-range plan in the past two years, much of your work has already been done for you. Lacking that, plan to do the needed self-study.

The self-study

As you begin to think through what is involved in the self-study, you will quickly realize that if your organization is large or even

HALF AS BIG
AND TWICE AS
RIGHTEOUS

Source: *Leadership,* Fall 1985, p. 52. Reprinted by permission of Doug Hall.

PASTORAL SEARCH COMMITTEE SURVEY
OF CALVARY BAPTIST CHURCH

We are asking for input from the Calvary Baptist Church family to help us
better understand our church. We also hope to identify some of the
qualities you are seeking in our new senior pastor.

You don't need to put your name on this survey, so please be completely
candid.

Please return completed surveys to the box on the information desk in the
narthex. If you prefer to mail it to church (2120 N. Lexington, 55113)
indicate "Attn: Pastoral Search Committee" on the envelope.

Please return surveys as soon as possible but NO LATER THAN JULY 26TH.

1. I have been attending Calvary Baptist for _____ years. I have been a
    member for _____ years.

2. Age _____   3. Male _____   Female _____   4. Single _____   Married _____

5. Over the last six months I've attended the following services on a
    monthly basis:

    Sunday Morning Worship   _____ times a month
    Sunday School   _____ times a month
    Sunday Evening Worship   _____ times a month
    Wednesday Evening   _____ times a month

6. The areas of church ministry that are most important to my spiritual
    life are: Check no more than 3 and number 1,2,3, in order of
    perceived need; 1 is high.

    [ ] preaching   [ ]   Christian fellowship
    [ ] worship services   [ ]   service opportunities
    [ ] Sunday school   [ ] children/youth activities
    [ ] prayer meeting   [ ]   other (please explain)

    _____

    _____

7. The spiritual need in my life that is not being met by Calvary Baptist
    Church is: _____

    _____

8. In my opinion, the 3 areas of Calvary Baptist Church which need the mos
    attention right now are: (do not list senior pastor).
    Prioritize by 1,2,3,; 1 is high.

    [ ] individual spiritual growth   serving one another [ ]
    [ ] outreach/witnessing/evangelism   prayer [ ]
    [ ] church unity/more love & patience   discipleship [ ]
    [ ] personal ministry involvement   vision for the future [ ]
    [ ] better communications from leaders   revival [ ]
    [ ] spiritual leadership   stewardship/tithing & giving [ ]
    [ ] other (please explain) _____

9. Indicate below the emphasis you think our church should place in each
   of the following areas:

	Emphasis About Right	Much More Needed	Somewhat More Needed	Less Emphasis Needed
Discipling new Christians	[ ]	[ ]	[ ]	[ ]
Caring for one another	[ ]	[ ]	[ ]	[ ]
Prayer - midweek service	[ ]	[ ]	[ ]	[ ]
Strengthening families	[ ]	[ ]	[ ]	[ ]
Communication to members	[ ]	[ ]	[ ]	[ ]
Bible teaching	[ ]	[ ]	[ ]	[ ]
Personal evangelism	[ ]	[ ]	[ ]	[ ]
Developing lay ministries	[ ]	[ ]	[ ]	[ ]
Friendship & hospitality	[ ]	[ ]	[ ]	[ ]
Small group meetings/homes	[ ]	[ ]	[ ]	[ ]
Pastoral counseling	[ ]	[ ]	[ ]	[ ]
Local outreach	[ ]	[ ]	[ ]	[ ]
Preaching	[ ]	[ ]	[ ]	[ ]
Senior citizen ministries	[ ]	[ ]	[ ]	[ ]
Financial stewardship	[ ]	[ ]	[ ]	[ ]
Sunday School	[ ]	[ ]	[ ]	[ ]
Youth programs	[ ]	[ ]	[ ]	[ ]
Childrens programs	[ ]	[ ]	[ ]	[ ]
Music programs	[ ]	[ ]	[ ]	[ ]
Missions	[ ]	[ ]	[ ]	[ ]
Athletic programs	[ ]	[ ]	[ ]	[ ]
Career Singles ministries	[ ]	[ ]	[ ]	[ ]
Worship service - morning	[ ]	[ ]	[ ]	[ ]
Worship service - evening	[ ]	[ ]	[ ]	[ ]
Other (please explain)	[ ]	[ ]	[ ]	[ ]

10. It's my opinion that the Sunday Morning Worship Services at Calvary
    Baptist Church should be:

    [ ]   More formal than they are
    [ ]   Just like they are now
    [ ]   Less formal than presently

    Comments:_____

11 The following are some of the qualities, abilities and interests the
    Pastoral Search Committee will consider in seeking a new senior pastor
    Indicate the 5 qualities you believe are the most important for our
    new pastor. Please number the 5 in order of priority 1,2,3,4,5; 1
    is high.

    [ ] Has strong devotional/prayer life   Is approachable [ ]
    [ ] Takes a strong stand on social issues   Is loving & caring [ ]
    [ ] Practices & teaches discipleship   Emphasizes missions [ ]
    [ ] Motivates church staff & lay leaders   Emphasizes evangelism [ ]
    [ ] Presently affiliated with BGC   Has the gift of preaching [ ]
    [ ] Provides applicable Bible teaching   Is a good administrator [ ]
    [ ] Is a strong, effective leader   Has a vision for the future [ ]
    [ ] Exhibits strong pastoral care qualities   Other-explain [ ]

12. Are there any other comments you would like to relay to the Pastoral
    Search Committee? (If you have recommendations for pastoral
    candidates please use the forms available at the information desk.)

    _____

of medium size, the study is going to take some effort and could consume two months of your time. Despite that, resist the temptation to cheat on this phase because this study is a needed building block for a successful outcome of the search effort.

The typical way to collect information is through questionnaires and interviews. In both cases the purpose is to find out how well the needs of the members are being met and to infer from that what to emphasize or de-emphasize in the future under the new leader. The questionnaire for those attending the church (nonmembers who attend regularly should be included) is really a consumer satisfaction survey and will have similarities to those you receive in the mail or those you get by telephone that ask why you bought—or didn't buy—their product.

Here is one survey that was used by a St. Paul, Minnesota church as part of their 1987 search for a new senior pastor. Calvary Baptist is a church of 700 members, affiliated with the Baptist General Conference and has an average Sunday morning attendance of 550.

If you go through the questions carefully, you will think of areas they seem to have forgotten. Yet they probably did not. If they had made the questionnaire any longer, it would have decreased the number of responses by intimidating the respondent. Calvary Baptist had 131 responses, which they felt gave them an adequate sampling. To try to include every member is not realistic, but if you can get 60-70 percent participation or more, be happy.

Someone from the search committee should interview the various groups of the church to see how they feel about the church, the adequacy of the various programs and what they hope for in a new pastor. At Calvary Baptist, only two respondents to the questionnaire were 19 years old or younger. That suggests a need to involve the young people and the leaders of the youth work in a more direct way. Similar interviews should be held with the missions committee, the church boards and any group whose input would be of value. Be careful not to offend by overlooking a group.

Loren B. Mead has written a fine booklet, *Critical Moment of Ministry.* In it, he says of self-studies,

Although I admire the collection and analysis of data, I do
get a bit nervous when people approach data with the fer-
vent look of a true believer. I really do not think you can
get much more than a good snapshot of reality, an impres-
sionistic sketch. Some people really seem to want to get
all of reality down in the tables and on the pages of the profile. I tend to prefer using skills of people (if you have
sophisticated people used to using sophisticated methods,
by all means use them!), but then wrestling with the
results—perhaps with feet up on the table. I think it is
very important in the self-study for lots of people in the
congregation to make input, but also for them to reflect on
what begins to emerge as the snapshot or sketch. In their
reflecting, they add new insights, they test the reality of
what is said, and they also identify with an emerging pic-
ture of who, indeed, they seem to be at this moment in
their history."[2]

Whether you use statistical data, personal intuition or a blend
of them, be sure you hear all the voices there are to be heard in
your organization.

The feedback
When you do a questionnaire, those who respond develop an
understandable desire to learn how their opinions fit those of
others. It makes good sense to provide feedback to the congregation after the responses have been tallied. Doing so lets them
know how they see themselves, their programs and their hopes
for the future. The report should also assist the members to
understand better that the criteria being used in the search for
the new pastor were shaped by their responses.

What questionnaires don't ask
Some aspects of a congregation's life are of crucial importance
but are so complex that they could not be included on a questionnaire to the congregation. Other issues must be left out because
the average person in the pew lacks an awareness of potential

problems in that area. For example, how well the pastor takes direction from the board, and vice versa, may be a major issue in a church where the departed pastor had a troubled board relationship. Input on that subject is needed by the search committee but is best obtained by interviews with board members.

My own church, Emmanuel Presbyterian, of Thousand Oaks, California, faces the need to replace the founding pastor when he retires. Over his 27 years of leadership the church has embraced both charismatic and noncharismatic believers in a cordial relationship under his loving guidance. During one period, the associate pastor was a charismatic also, but the charismatic members never saw the exercise of New Testament gifts as a basis for feeling spiritually superior, so no rifts developed in the congregation.

In seeking a new pastor, it will be essential for our church to find someone who also will warmly embrace charismatic members and focus the attention of all members on those things that bind them together rather than on those that could become divisive. However, the issue is too complex to deal with in a questionnaire, and many members would not even know what the terminology meant.

Denominational assistance

If your church is part of a denomination, see what assistance denominational headquarters can provide you as you do your self-study. Many denominations have a well-developed hierarchy, such as the Reformed Church in America (RCA) or the Presbyterian Church (U.S.A.), and you will find they expect you to fill out extensive forms before they will send you the data you need on available candidates.

The six-page RCA Church Profile Form that is reproduced for you (see Appendix 1) will give you a good start on your self-study. The Presbyterian 12-page form (see Appendices 2 and 3) is helpful, too, but will also test your patience and forbearance.

These forms help your group see who you are, where you may wish to go in the future and what type of a leader you are seeking to take you there. Also, they are used to encourage or direct you to follow the policies and procedures your denomination feels are important.

In turn, the information your church provides your denomination is needed by them as they try to recommend for your consideration the candidates who will best fit your needs.

After you know with confidence who you are now, the next question is: Where does your group want to go in the future?

Where Are We Going?

After you know with confidence who you are now, the next question is: Where does your group want to go in the future? If you cannot answer that question, it is not fair to invite a new pastor or president to be your leader. Lead you where? should be the question the candidate asks of you.

The starting point for answering the question of where the organization is going is to reexamine the mission statement of the organization. If you do not have such a document, perhaps this is the time to develop one. If the reexamination of your mission statement reveals that it is out-of-date or otherwise now inappropriate, recasting it now is timely so that it points your organization in the correct direction even before you begin inviting someone to lead it.

Organizations, including churches, have a maturation cycle that should be considered as the future is visualized. If you have just completed a major growth in numbers, now could be the time to build a larger facility to accommodate them, or it may be time to find leadership that will emphasize the spiritual dimension. Or, if the membership has slipped a lot under the prior pastor, you may need to stabilize things financially under a leader who can operate well under budgetary constraints. In a college or Bible school setting, you may be at a state where fundraising, raising the academic standards or increasing enrollment is the pressing need.

As your committee seeks to discern the future, the ques-

tionnaire to the congregation can be of some help but probably
only a little. What a congregation wants may be quite different
from what it needs or what it can afford. The board is normally
best equipped to determine where things should be going and
often an informed denominational executive can be of great
value.

---

*Aggressive faith, while a little scary, feels
exhilarating and superspiritual as we dare to
"risk all for Christ." I suggest this kind of
derring-do is best left to the visionary leader.*

Christians are a people of faith and we sometimes allow our
enthusiasm to mingle with our awareness of God's riches and
"promises" so that we build a set of expectations that are pre-
destined to fail. Church growth experts can identify the factors
that are associated with a congregation that grows or fails. While
God can do something very special, if He chooses to, most
churches follow certain principles that relate to demographic factors, financial resources and leadership. If a search committee
prays hard and is full of enthusiasm but lacks even a modicum of
experience and does not seek wise counsel, it may plot a future
that is unrealistic. And unrealistic expectation leads to disappointment and even to possible disillusion.

It is interesting to speculate whether faith, wrongly understood, can become so extreme or excessive as to be presumptuous. As Americans, we tend to view growth and bigness as
"success," while, as Christians, we frequently interpret those
same factors as evident signs of God's blessing. Aggressive
faith, while a little scary, feels exhilarating and superspiritual as
we dare to "risk all for Christ." I suggest this kind of derring-do
is best left to the visionary leader, not to the search committee
preparing the road map for the new leader. My personal feeling
is that bigness per se is no evidence of God's blessing. A review
of the growth and retrenchment of any number of Christian organizations gives ample proof of this fact.

How far and by when?

Determining the direction in which you wish to go is only the first step in planning the future of your church. You also need to consider just how far you want to go in that direction—and by when? Difficult though it may be for you to do so, you need to try to answer these questions.

When you have a congregation that lacks consensus on where to go or you have an angry group full of recriminations, you may not be able to arrive at definite answers. How much simpler it is when the charter is for a pastor to build a strong Christian education program or for the college president to be given two years to restore the institution to a balanced budget. Clearly, some desired goals cannot be put into numbers, but others can be, and the effort should be made to do so.

Sharing the vision

Your plan for your organization is the vision you will hope to communicate to your candidates. If they feel your expectations are excessive, they may tell you so or will withdraw from consideration. That may be your committee's first clue that your plans lack realism.

But the reverse is also possible. You may lose good candidates because they see your vision as too timid and lacking in faith. In that case, you will probably attract a candidate with modest aspirations, thereby assuring a good match but a dull future.

So whose vision is it?

Is the board the custodian of the vision of the ministry, or is the leader? As I see it, the board—the legal owner of the enterprise—has the responsibility to preserve and nurture that enterprise. But board members seldom do anything with that organization's vision except select the leader and then approve or disapprove the leader's actions and recommendations.

Why is this so? My experience is that board members usually are not visionaries themselves. Rather, they are the supporters, advisors and even critics of the leader who provides the vision. I have seen few boards able to clearly set out for the can-

didate an exciting road map of the future of their church, college
or parachurch group. The most they seem to do is to review
where they have come from and are now, while pointing to the
future with few specifics but lots of hope. Such a board usually
hires the person who does the best job of painting for them a
vision of future ministry that fits their hopes and who seems the
most likely one to bring it about.

Seldom have I seen a board press the leader to try new programs. The initiative invariably comes from the leader. The
president or the pastor is the one who usually feels the leading of
God to try a new ministry or who senses an opportunity to serve
in a new or expanded way. The leader then generates support
and enthusiasm from the board, if he can, for his new idea. If his
proposals are turned down regularly, he will feel a lack of support and leave. On the other hand, if the board supports him, but
his programs fail, they then ask him to leave.

The shared vision

If your experience confirms mine, you will also see that the
board guards and protects the vision of the ministry while the
pastor/president energizes it. True, he can modify it and—with
their permission—does so, usually quite gradually. But ulti-
mately, it is a shared vision. If the leader and the board begin to
see different emphases or even want to take different routes to
get to the same shared goal, problems will arise, and then something has to give. Only when leader and board clearly see the
same vision, can things go well for the institution.

Invariably, the shared vision is the one with the greatest
hope of becoming reality.

Notes
1. Reprinted by permission of Neil Whitehouse, chairman, Pastoral Search
Committee, Calvary Baptist Church, St. Paul, Minnesota.
2. Loren B. Mead, "Self-Study," *Critical Moments of Ministry: A Change of
Pastors,* p. 23. Reprinted by permission from The Alban Institute, Inc., 4125
Nebraska Avenue, NW, Washington, DC 20016. Copyright 1986. All rights
reserved.

CHAPTER FIVE

WHAT DO WE WANT IN OUR LEADER?

UNFORTUNATELY, we tend to want everything we can think of. However, very, very seldom do we find a candidate who can meet all our criteria. Your search committee will surely start out listing every personal quality and type of experience they could want, but it is vital that they pare the list down to the few essentials that the candidate must have. In some areas they must be willing to settle for average competence and even to accept weaknesses in others.

Strengths vs. Weaknesses

Dr. Peter Druckcr, the famous management consultant, told a seminar of Christian leaders, "You can only be effective with your strengths, not your weaknesses. Match your strengths and tasks."[1] Thus, your committee must find candidates whose strengths parallel the primary needs of your organization at this time.

Dr. Drucker adds, "Jesus did very few things. He healed and preached. He didn't even pick a successor."[2] No search committee would settle for a candidate who only did two things well, would they? Without doubt, we tend today to ask too much initially of the candidates. But as a number of them are interviewed, the committee begins to see that its expectations are excessive.

Dr. Drucker has another observation on leadership that will convert into an interviewing tip for your committee. He says, "What you would like to do is not a reliable guide to what you do well. But what you *don't* like correlates highly with what you do poorly."[3]

A responsible search committee will protect a candidate against noble but self-destructive inclinations by restricting the number of hours to be put in by their new leader.

So, if you need a new college president who can raise substantial new funds, don't assume a candidate can do it well if he says he likes the task. Perhaps he can, but you cannot be certain. A genuine liking for fund-raising allows for the possibility of success, while there is no possibility of it if the candidate dislikes this type of work. Take heed of Peter Drucker's wisdom.

How Much Is Too Much?

We have examined the desire that a candidate be great at everything and how unrealistic that expectation is. If you agree to accept limitations in some areas of a candidate's ability, you still will want him to make a good effort in all areas of the job. For a pastor, that usually means preaching, teaching, visitation, counseling, performing marriages and funerals, administrating, engaging in community activities and undertaking a number of other tasks that vary from place to place.

How much work is too much for your leader? I'm sure you wouldn't settle for a 40-hour week for your leader. But how many hours would you consider to be fair? Your search committee should be cautious that what you expect from your new leader doesn't amount to being a killer of a job.

"We're looking for someone with a doctorate in
Christian education and five years of experience,
but we'll settle for someone with a van."

Source: *Leadership*, Summer 1987, p. 91. Reprinted by permission of Steve Phelps.

Bob Buford, the Texas TV executive and foundation president with deep interest in Christian leadership, says, "A major problem [with Christian leadership] is losing touch with your holiness by getting too busy with ministry."[4]

Ministry candidates are almost too willing to take on challenges that are excessively demanding. Their dedication to serving Christ can cause them to work so hard that burnout takes place and marriage problems develop because so little time is spent with the family. A responsible search committee will protect a candidate against noble but self-destructive inclinations by restricting the number of hours to be put in by their new leader. In Appendix 4 is a description of a typical workweek, written 20 years ago by Rev. Robert Roxburgh, yet it still has applicability today.

Unusual Candidates

Your church is probably one of those which, like most, has been served for many years by a male pastor who was married and had a family. Today's ministers are a different group than those of 20 or 30 years ago because times have changed. Is your church or college willing to consider nontraditional candidates? Let's discuss what these might be.

Female ministers/leaders: While some denominations have not ordained women, many have, and many able candidates are available because of the difficulty they are finding in obtaining senior positions.

During 1987, Eastern College, a Baptist institution in St. Davids, Pennsylvania, hired Dr. Roberta Hestenes, an ordained Presbyterian minister and educator as president, making her the first female president of a Christian college.

Co-pastors: In some churches two pastors share the total responsibility instead of having a senior pastor and an associate pastor.

The husband/wife ministry team: Co-pastors, consisting of an ordained husband-and-wife team, are becoming more accepted in some circles.

Ethnic minority candidates: Though a perceptible trend exists toward a broader basis of selection from minorities, it still is most common for white churches to have white pastors, black churches to have black pastors and so on.

Equal opportunity hiring: Some denominations insist that search committees subscribe to equal opportunity guidelines. They say something to this effect: "The Committee on Ministry shall provide for the implementation of equal opportunity employment for ministers and candidates without regard to race, ethnic origin, sex, age, or marital status."

The phrase, "different theological positions" can cause controversy in a denomination as pluralistic as the Presbyterian (U.S.A.) church. A recent edict by the denomination adds, "marital status" to the list of leader qualifications, a concern which would be hard for many churches to handle. Your church must decide if it will consider candidates who are separated, divorced or remarried. Overlooking "sexual preference" as a basis for discrimination in hiring is common now in the public sector, but this view has not yet been accepted in evangelical groups, though some mainline denominations now have a running battle on this issue of allowing practicing homosexuals to be in active ministry.

Other factors that do not fall under equal opportunity guidelines also enter into hiring decisions.

- Would you hire a candidate whose wife was slovenly in appearance or very overweight?
- Would you consider seriously a candidate who has a Down's Syndrome child?
- If your candidate has a child undergoing drug dependency therapy, would you consider him?
- Is a candidate acceptable who had cancer surgery two years ago?

As you wrestle with the possibility of nontraditional candidates, your committee must consider applicable Scripture, denominational guidelines and those factors that your congregation could accept in a leader without becoming divided. I wish you well in your deliberations.

However formidable biblical standards may seem, they are the starting point, the basic building blocks for what you should look for in your new leader.

Scriptural Standards

Every search committee for a Christian ministry must begin with Scripture as the selection criteria are developed. I recall how being confronted by the New Testament standards intimidated me when I was asked to serve as an elder in my church. However formidable biblical standards may seem, they are the starting point, the basic building blocks for what you should look for in your new leader.

In 1970, Leonard E. Hill reviewed the New Testament standards for pastors. Here is his list:

Outward Reputation

Have a good reputation even when his life is lived as an open book (1 Tim. 3:2; Titus 1:7).

Be well thought of, even by those outside the church (1 Tim. 3:7).

Be irreproachable in his marital relations (1 Tim. 3:2; Titus 1:6).

In other words, a pastor is to be a man who has a good reputation in his church, in society and in his home.

Inner Disposition

Not selfish, quick-tempered, intemperate, violent or

overly interested in material things (1 Tim. 3:3; Titus 1:7).

Have a love for people and for that which is good (1 Tim. 3:2; Titus 1:8).

Be sensible, mature, well-balanced and self-controlled (1 Tim. 3:2; Titus 1:8).

Be Christlike and devoted to God (Titus 1:8).

A pastor with the right kind of inner disposition should have right attitudes toward himself and toward God and should reflect Christian maturity.

Christian Experience

Not a novice or new convert (1 Tim. 3:6).

Prove himself faithful and able to guide others by managing his own household well; should have believing and obedient children (1 Tim. 3:4; Titus 1:6).

Be a skillful teacher (1 Tim. 3:2), one who has been taught what is true and knows how to teach it to others (Titus 1:9).[5]

Other Factors to Consider

In addition to the scriptural standards, the other factors to consider are primarily tied to the duties listed in the position description. But additional concerns can also be involved.

Would it be wise to choose a candidate with an urban background for a rural Montana church? Before you rush to a quick answer, I mention my own pastor, who has had 28 years of outstanding ministry after starting a church in a suburban southern California community with prior experience only in tiny Post Falls, Idaho. So don't rule out the growth potential of your candidates in your deliberations.

Your church has a cultural flavor that needs to be considered as you develop your selection criteria. I'm not referring as much to doctrinal or denominational distinctives as to those related to locale, the economic level or the educational level of the congregation and other similar factors. Also, consider the music preferences of your congregation and how a candidate would relate to them.

Another factor to be considered, perhaps a cultural consideration as well, is the leadership style that the organization or congregation has been accustomed to. Whether your group has had a strong, authoritative style of leadership or an easy going participative one, consideration should be given to how well that style was received and how things prospered under that style of leadership. If everything went well, thought should be given to continuing that style under the new leader. If it went badly, perhaps a new type of leader is called for.

Various church groups offer lists of things to be considered by search committees. The General Association of Regular Baptists (GARB) offers such a list. These three items are from that list:

> His control over his children.
> Does he pay his bills and handle money properly?
> Is he well liked by other pastors?

Another one from the GARB list strikes a different, less-strategic note:

> His wife's housekeeping.

Really?

Your committee needs to build its own list of matters to inquire into. Many of the questions that arise can be answered through reference checking, covered in depth in chapter 10.

The Position Description

Your new leader needs to have a written description of what you expect him to do. Even before that, your search committee needs to prepare one so that you agree on what your needs are. It will not be difficult to prepare, if you have done your self-study. In any case, you need it to show to a candidate to let him know what you expect of him. If you develop a performance evaluation for your new leader, the position description is the base on which it can be built.

If you presently do not have a position description for the role you are seeking to fill, you probably can prepare one most easily by looking at someone else's and modifying it to fit your needs. Why reinvent the wheel? In Appendix 2 you will find a form from the Presbyterian Church (U.S.A.) that lists 20 pastoral activities. It covers most of the things you will want to include.

Also, in Appendix 5 is a "Recruitment Profile" that I used in the search for the president of InterVarsity Christian Fellowship. While not appropriate for a pastoral search, it was suitable for use with a parachurch organization or college.

How Am I Doing?

The well-informed candidate will request your search committee to provide not only a job description and the goals of the organization, but also some system of evaluating his performance annually. Any employee has the right to know how well he is doing, even pastors and presidents. Board members who plan to do their job well should insist on a performance evaluation system.

How can salary increases be fairly made unless they are related to how well the job is being done? Similarly, how can corrective influences be applied to a leader who has no standards by which to measure his work? Your board should view their role as including the responsibility to assist in your leader's professional development. A performance evaluation system provides the best basis for doing that.

You will agree that it is unfair to fire a leader if he has had no prior awareness that things were going badly. But it happens and more likely so in situations where no performance review system exists. When the system is absent, the pressure builds until an eruption takes place, and things then are often beyond the point of no return. While a performance evaluation requires some tough love at times, it is biblical, psychologically desirable

PRESIDENTIAL PERFORMANCE REVIEW

We are concerned to learn your opinion of the leadership that the president is bringing to MAF. In performance reviews you are not being asked to reveal the final word on leadership qualities, but to provide us with your perception of the degree to which you feel the current president is carrying out the responsibilities of the office as outlined in his job description. The effectiveness of the review depends upon your willingness to share your views as candidly as possible. The purpose of the review is not to grade the president but to help the board as it works with the president toward supporting the MAF team as it carries out its God-given task.

Please respond to each statement according to the following number code:
1. Strongly disagree
2. Disagree
3. No definite opinion
4. Agree
5. Strongly agree

Where you feel that you have no basis for a response please use #3. The same number will serve in cases where you are informed but neither agree nor disagree. Circle the number which most accurately expresses your opinion regarding the work of the president. Annotate the statement if you feel it needs to be clarified.

1 2 3 ④ 5   (1) Has developed and articulated a clear mission for MAF.

1 2 ③ 4 5   (2) Has developed strong ties with churches, other missions and international leadership.

1 2 3 ④ 5   (3) Is a skillful organizer of people.

1 2 3 ④ 5   (4) Has demonstrated wisdom in selecting people to serve on his leadership team.

1 2 3 ④ 5   (5) Tends to make a decision only after hearing the opinions of those affected by the decision.

1 2 3 4 ⑤   (6) Is concerned for the spiritual development of the entire organization.

1 2 3 ④ 5   (7) Shares his goals for MAF with all members of the organization.

1 2 3 ④ 5   (8) The recent reorganization was primarily his own idea.

1 2 ③ 4 5   (9) Has demonstrated the ability to develop his subordinates.

1 2 3 ④ 5   (10) Has a vision for MAF which is moving us rapidly toward an even more exciting future.

1 2 3 ④ 5   (11) Tends away from an increasingly bureaucratic organization.

1 2 3 ④ 5   (12) Has the confidence of the majority of those in MAF.

1 2 3 ④ 5   (13) Does not object to personnel having contact with Board members.

1 2 ③ 4 5   (14) Is interested in hearing the opinions of others regardless of their place in the organization.

1 2 3 4 ⑤   (15) I would be pleased to see him continue as president of MAF.

1 2 3 ④ 5   (16) Is willing to delegate work to others.

1 2 ③ 4 5   (17) Holds people accountable for reaching goals.

1 2 3 4 ⑤   (18) MAF is a better organization today than it was before he came.

Please comment on what you think is MAF's biggest problem today. Also, what is its greatest opportunity.

Signature (optional)
Note: All responses will be maintained in strictest confidence. 7

and a good management practice.

When your leader is doing well, or even superbly, the time for the performance evaluation is a delightful experience, a time to say to your leader what we all hope to hear someday, "Well done, thou good and faithful servant" (Matt. 25:21).

The best evaluation process possible for your organization is one devised by you to meet your needs. If you need some suggestions to get started, read the Alban Institute's publication, *Evaluation: Of, By, For and To the Clergy* by Loren B. Mead.[6] Here is a simple process that was used by Mission Aviation Fellowship for their first presidential evaluation (see the following document). Adapted and modified to your own requirements, it will undoubtedly work well for your organization, too.

By the time you and your committee have worked your way through these various steps, you will have a firm idea of both what you want *in* your new leader and what you will want *from* him.

Notes
1. "Drucker on Leadership" in "Musings of the Sage," *Reflections from the Lamp* 3 Winter 1987):1.
2. Peter Drucker at Peter Drucker Management Seminar, La Verne, CA, October 1, 1978.
3. "Drucker on Leadership," p. 1.
4. Bob Buford in comments made at Christian Leadership Seminar, 1987.
5. Leonard E. Hill, *Your Work on the Pulpit Committee* (Nashville: Broadman Press, 1970), p. 44. All rights reserved. Used by permission.
6. Loren B. Mead, *Evaluation: Of, By, For and To the Clergy*. Published by The Alban Institute, Inc., 4125 Nebraska Avenue, NW, Washington, DC 20016. Copyright 1977. All rights reserved.
7. Used by permission of Dr. Robert H. Mounce.

CHAPTER SIX
PUTTING YOUR BEST FOOT FORWARD

THOSE of us in the recruiting profession know that we need to gain a candidate's interest by telling everything attractive about the proffered position that we can think of. To a lesser extent, you do the same as you seek to fill your need for a pastor or president. However, you must be careful not to emphasize money, a choice location or other inducements that sound unspiritual. That could turn off the deeply spiritual candidate that you want.

Preparing Your Data

As you prepare data on your church for candidates to consider, you will fill out the form provided by your denomination. Sample forms are found in the back of the book (see Appendices 1 and 3). That's necessary and a good starting point but I encourage you to be creative and go beyond that. You must find a balance in the material you prepare between your optimistic hopes for your church and a realistic and coldly factual assessment of where you now are.

In Christian circles, I find that most choice servants of the Lord are interested in demanding situations that will stretch them, but less-committed people may respond to an easier, plush type of position. I should add, however, that candidates who respond to these tougher challenges still want to know that the job can be done. No intelligent candidate wants to step into a crushing debt load, a deeply divided church or other conditions that virtually assure failure.

I see no reason not to put the best light possible on the situation your organization is in, consistent with the facts. Obviously, Christians need to be truthful, so that is the starting point. Beyond that, if a candidate finds a discernible gap between what you have said and what he learns when he visits with you, you can expect him to drop out of consideration. So beware of excessive enthusiasm that will make your material seem full of hype.

Wooing the Candidates

When your interest as a search committee focuses on a few promising candidates you should be prepared to put on your "full-court press." You should share whatever materials you can devise that will tell the candidate who you are and what your vision for ministry is. These would certainly include several annual church reports, some Sunday bulletins and other materials that will give him a feel for the life of the church. In this video age, the following idea could be a useful one, I believe:

> Find someone in your congregation who has a videotape camera and can use it reasonably well. Or, hire a professional. Have him do a tape covering your physical facilities. Add to that a few minutes on the tape with key church leaders and have them share their hopes for the church. You may want to add a few people, such as a spokesman for the youth group, who may not be an elected church leader. I predict that such an introduction will do well in presenting your case, if your people can be fairly natural on camera.
>
> If it is possible, also put on your tape some footage that allows the candidate to get a sample of your music pro-

"I understand there's a strong faction in the church."

Source: *Leadership,* Summer 1985, p. 83. Reprinted by permission of Howard Parris.

gram. Interviews with others on the pastoral staff could also be used, if you feel it will be a selling point. The reproducing of this tape is not expensive and is simple to do. Any candidate either has a VCR or has access to one so it should be no problem to play your tape.

Rare is the candidate who will want to consider your need if his family resolutely opposes a move. If a spouse is loudly complaining and the kids are stewing, hearing God's voice of guidance over the sounds of domestic battle can be difficult.

You may wish to add a few items of interest for other members of the family. Where I have had families that enjoy outdoor recreation, I have sought out paperback books that describe the many vacation opportunities. I found this tactic helpful, for instance, in the states of Washington and Wisconsin. When the opportunity was in southern California and involved a Massachusetts family, I sent along Disneyland materials to develop the interest of the children.

The material on the church will catch the interest of the candidate. After all, it's his career. But his wife may need other interests to get her excited about living in the new area, and certainly the children have that need. Rare is the candidate who will want to consider your need if his family resolutely opposes a move. If your efforts lessen family resistance, you have allowed the candidate to consider your service opportunity by eliminating hampering home constraints. If a spouse is loudly complaining and the kids are stewing, hearing God's voice of guidance over the sounds of domestic battle can be difficult.

How Can This Be Spiritual?

It may occur to you that the more you try to sell a candidate and his family on your opening, the less room you are leaving for the Holy Spirit to influence him. You may have a point there. Cer-

tainly you need to avoid appealing to wrong instincts in a candidate. Yet it is also important to let him know about the ministry
place you have open. Have you ever heard of anyone feeling a
call to serve God in a place they haven't heard of? Yes, some
"selling" can be appropriate, I believe.

If your church is located in Carmel, California or your college
is in Boca Raton, Florida, you have a special problem. Your location is so choice that you may find a candidate being interested in
your opening for the wrong reasons. The other side of the coin
is that a candidate may decline interest, because he fears considering this opportunity for less-than-spiritual reasons. You should
be prepared to counter such a concern or at least help him work
through the problem.

> I once had a reverse type of problem in a secular search
> assignment. Our challenge was to find someone who
> would take a position in the depressing mining town of
> Butte, Montana. We flew the candidates in at night and
> hustled them off in the dark to a lovely lodge outside of
> town. Breakfast was held there with key people so that
> the candidates would be focused on the job challenge
> before they were allowed to see the open-pit town.

Perhaps such a ploy strikes you as unacceptable, but the
purpose was to focus on the opportunity, not on the negatives
which could be dealt with later. You may face a need to be creative, too, in your search effort. Your challenge may involve problems such as location, compensation, church finances, housing
or other matters.

Regional Attitudes

As your search committee members get to know each other,
you may be surprised to find that a whole range of biases exist in
you and in your fellow members. You may find attitudes suggesting that certain regional accents would not be well received. You
you may find feelings voiced that people from certain areas
"won't fit in."

These attitudes on the part of your committee members

have a reverse side, depending on where you are located. If you are in the Seattle area, be ready to counter negative thoughts about the climate. If you are in Houston, be ready to discuss the economy and weather. In California, it's the reputation for kooky people, and in southern California, it's smog. Whatever the bad rap is on your area, be ready to counter it.

When Your Best Foot Forward Isn't Very Good

If your church is healthy, growing and has been a happy, continuing love feast, skip this segment. It doesn't apply to you. But some colleges, parachurch groups or churches are in a real mess. No matter how you try to dress things up, the problems are simply enormous and are likely to intimidate most candidates. Several examples come to mind:

- A denominational college has had a leadership crisis that shortly led to a financial crisis.
- A parachurch organization grew beyond the abilities of its aging, longtime president who had become indecisive and stoutly resisted the idea of retiring.
- A church brought in a new pastor with the challenge to get the church growing again—but the lay leaders retained power and would not cooperate in making needed changes to create a growth-producing environment.
- The congregation of an urban church is now mostly older folks, the youth have largely gone elsewhere and racial minorities have moved heavily into the area the church serves.
- An international parachurch ministry has removed its president for ineptness and lack of financial responsibility. Great concern exists over conditions overseas, contributions are dropping sharply, and designated donor funds have been used for other purposes.

These are just a few true situations I have seen where a leader was needed who could turn a bad situation around or who could step in to quickly save a bad situation from becoming a certified disaster. There *are* a few people who can do these remarkable tasks. Some people recognize their special aptitude for doing these dirty jobs well and are attracted to them. To find such a rare talent you must do two things, neither of which is easy:

1. Recognize that your "turn around" leader may not be the person who will be your long-term leader.
2. Recognize that to attract the qualified person to clean things up, you must be candid in discussing your needs, as distressing as that may be.

In the business world the turn-around specialists are a tough, talented bunch who know how to ferret out problems, shut down unprofitable operations, dispose of unprofitable product lines and give liberal doses of strong medicine to save the company. They are decisive, strong people who never lose their focus on saving the company, if it is possible. To them, being unpopular is almost expected and confrontation is a daily occurrence.

A quick review of these qualities will let you realize that these are not leadership qualities that we value highly in religious circles. Most Christian leaders deliberately seek to avoid developing such qualities, and they are usually pretty successful at it. (I find the ability to confront problems and the willingness to be held accountable to performance standards to be a glaring deficiency among Christian leaders.)

If you need a leader who is decisive, can resolve conflicts, be a significant change agent and do well in an adverse climate, you are looking for a special person. You must be willing to "tell it like it is" to candidates. It is impossible to find such a person without revealing your needs for what they are.

I am aware of numerous situations where boards failed to be frank and brought in unsuspecting new leaders who, in each case, were dismayed when they found out the true situation, were unequipped to handle it—and failed. Sometimes, the responsible people failed to see their situation realistically and innocently set the stage for failure of the new leader. In other situations, opposing factions, out of spite, sandbagged the leader by causing the failure of the person selected by "the other group." As unchristian and savage as that sounds, if you have observed many Christian organization leadership situations, I suspect you have also seen such embarrassing, deplorable situations.

Turn-around leaders aren't as lovable as we typically like. The stern stuff of which they are made cause them to be seen as "too strong" for the more placid groups. These pilots who steer through rough or treacherous waters also can get bored easily in tranquil situations. All of this means that these people may not care to stay or to linger after the tough work is done. Thus, you should anticipate that another search may be needed when things are restored to an even keel. A crisis manager doesn't fit a noncrisis situation. Also, the price of confrontation is often the loss of popularity that is needed to hold on to a job in a church setting.

When a group of Christians want desperately to find an organizational savior, the biblical pattern usually is played out to its grisly conclusion. That is, the new "savior" is initially reverenced, later renounced and then crucified.

A good search for such a turn-around type of person begins with the candor to describe the troubled situation and see who has previously succeeded in a similar situation and is willing to try again.

The Candidate Looks Behind the Facade

When your search committee interviews a candidate, you typically tell all the positive things first. That's what the candidate does, too, as he reveals himself to you. The negatives, the limitations, the problems come later when either a sense of mutual trust builds or when incisive questions become acceptable after getting acquainted. The search committee has a big advantage in the give-and-take of the interviews. Not only are there more of them, but they have a carefully crafted agenda that they do not share at the start of things with the candidate.

The candidate needs to be alert and resourceful to get all he needs to know from a search committee that has something they wish to hide. When he senses a hidden agenda or a tension among the committee members, he needs to get some answers if he is to have continuing interest in being a candidate. His career can suffer irreparable damage if he fails to ask strategic questions and gets involved in a no-win situation. Here are some ways a candidate can find the truth when he believes the committee is holding back what he needs to know.

- Contact the prior pastor/president.
- Ask denomination officials for a detailed rundown.
- Closely examine the records for evidence of high turnover of pastors and staff, declining income, falling attendance and so on.
- Don't let one person on the committee do all the talking. Get the quiet ones to respond to your thoughtful questions. Also, arrange for talking to some members individually and look for problem areas. Do you find substantial disagreement?
- Try to understand the power structure of the organization and the decision-making process.
- Avoid wanting the position so much that it colors your gathering of needed facts. Stay cool and objective!
- Get the committee members to list the successes and failures of the previous leader.
- What salary adjustments were made annually for the former leader?

The Disillusion Curve

When a new leader comes in there are high expectations, evident good will and usually lots of enthusiasm. Both the new leader and the search committee feel this way and it spreads to the board and then to those to be led.

That's good! That's the way it should be, *unless* the expectations are excessive on either side.

I am amazed by the arrogance and resulting lack of realism on the part of some search committees. They start out wanting it all! In their eagerness and self-delusion they seem to seek:

- the good looks of Dr. Lloyd Ogilvie;
- the scholarship of Dr. John Stott;
- the certainty of Dr. John MacArthur;
- the enthusiasm of Dr. Bruce Larson;
- the ability of a Rev. Bill Hybels to get a church to grow;
- the fund-raising skills of Dr. Norman Edwards;
- the humility of my pastor, Rev. Roger Meriwether;
- the administrative skills of Campus Crusade's Steve Douglass;
- the counseling skills of Dr. Jim Dobson;
- the marvelous Scottish accent of Rev. Tom Houston, former president of World Vision International; as well as
- the crowning asset, a wife such as Sharol Hayner, spouse of the president of InterVarsity Christian Fellowship.

Even if such a person existed—and none does—why would such a person be willing to talk to your group?

Expecting too much leads inevitably to disappointment and disillusionment. My "disillusion curve" is a graph of the drop in confidence that follows the hiring, if the expectations were unrealisticly high. Notice in the following chart that, four months after being hired, the same person, performing just as before, can be viewed quite differently, depending on what the initial expectations were.

The letdown, resulting from excessive expectations, is inevitable and very difficult to recover from. Strangely, such overly inflated hopes are seldom because of a misrepresentation by the candidate or the church. Rather, it's because both parties failed to make a careful exploration of what they wanted and hoped for—and by when.

The fateful disillusion curve can be avoided by a ruthless self-

CONFIDENCE LEVEL CHART

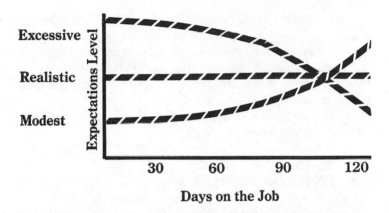

examination and disclosure by both parties. Deceitfulness or laziness in probing the details of mutual expectations, on the other hand, will bring on the disturbing diseases that accompany the disillusion curve.

When a group of Christians want desperately to find an organizational savior, the biblical pattern usually is played out to its grisly conclusion. That is, the new "savior" is initially reverenced, later renounced and then crucified. It's an unholy parallel to the truly redemptive story of the New Testament. But this latter-day version fails, even in this strained analogy, because there are no more sinless leaders to hang, even on organizational or institutional crosses, and a resurrection is unthinkable.

Mapping the Minefield

I recall the beautiful April day in 1945 when, as a young serviceman, I sat in my jeep, looking admiringly over a lovely German meadow. While I was enjoying the view, my eye caught a sign that said, *Achtung: Minen* (Attention: Mines). Immediately, my whole attitude changed, and our platoon avoided going across that field full of hidden mines. Applying the analogy is unpleasant, when we think of any Christian church, college or parachurch group as having within them people or situations that can blow up or damage the ministry of an unwary new leader. Nevertheless, I think it is true in more situations than we care to acknowledge.

Consequently, an enormously useful tool for the new leader is a map that warns him of dangers he might possibly encounter and that also provides keys to successful programs and relationships within the group. The departing leader could assist his successor in a major way by leaving such a legacy for him. And if he doesn't do so, someone else should.

What is on this map? Such items as a "hot issues" list of topics with potential for conflict, such as:

- inerrancy,
- the National Council of Churches,
- the new organ the church recently purchased,
- remarriage of divorced persons,
- ordination of women,
- tithing.

You get the idea. Your new leader can function better if he knows where scar tissue remains from earlier conflicts and can then use such information to shape his understanding of God's Word in his preaching.

The church leadership of the present and recent past should be identified—in the church pictorial directory, if one is available. What are their gifts? Do they get things done? and What are their interpersonal skills? These are the kinds of information that can be useful. Also, who are the probable troublemakers? and What gets them agitated? are concerns an incoming leader needs to know.

If the college has a board member or alumnus who expects coddling because of his significant donations, that is important to know. If the former pastor was asked to leave, it is helpful to the new leader to know who of influence may be fighting a rearguard action on his behalf.

Happily, the legacy will also have a list of people who can be counted on in special situations, such as these:

- "Mr. Johnson is a wise counselor, absolutely discreet and

understands the tensions of being a pastor."
- "Mr. and Mrs. McDaniel are usually agreeable to funding youth projects in the $1,000 to $2,000 range."
- "When the college has organizational problems, contact Mr. MacKenzie who has rich experience in that area."
- "If you need clout at denominational headquarters, talk to Mrs. Demarest whose father was for years a key leader there. She knows everyone and is well respected."

Such tips to facilitate congregational life will assist the new pastor substantially.

Lyle E. Schaller, in his book, *The Pastor and the People,* draws on his rich experience as a parish consultant when he speaks of leaving a legacy for the next leader. He advises including in that legacy written records of financial history and details of successful/unsuccessful programs along with active and inactive membership lists, information about parishioners who need special help, attendance records and a who's who of neighboring pastors. He also suggests that the departing leader leave an account of "my six best successes and six biggest defeats."

If the outgoing leader has had a successful ministry and is leaving in an outpouring of fond recollections, it is fully appropriate for him to invest the necessary time to prepare this road map for the person who will now be taking on the leadership. If the leaving has been acrimonious and abrupt, the need may be even greater, though finding the Christian grace to do it will be harder. Yet the road map he leaves may provide the keys that will enable the next leader to be more successful. Any leader with a high sense of ministry or churchmanship will find time to undertake this chore, even if doing so is painful.

So, yes, do put your best foot forward. But as you do so in your search for a heaven-sent leader, keep that foot firmly planted on the solid ground of realistic expectations, forthright honesty and prudent foresight by making use of the suggestions presented here.

CHAPTER SEVEN

LOOKING FOR THE CANDIDATES

B Y now your search committee should be getting impatient to see some live candidates. "Where are they? Let's get them in here and start interviewing," is the prevailing mood at this point. Where you go looking for candidates depends a lot on who you are. Let's discuss first the situation faced by a church searching for a senior pastor—in a small church that's the *only* pastor.

Working Within the Denomination
In denominationally connected churches, it is normal to call the regional headquarters and ask for help. If you are Presbyterian, you have already filled out forms and have had an advisor appointed to work with you. Based on the forms you filled out, headquarters will have files or dossiers sent to you on candidates who best meet the criteria you established. Depending upon your criteria, you may get from 25 to 100 such files for your review. But the quantity can vary a lot, relative to the supply-and-demand balance in your denomination between available clergy vacant pulpits.

If you are a congregation of the Church of the Nazarene, Christian and Missionary Alliance, Foursquare Gospel or any of numerous others, you will find your denomination wants to do most of the search committee's work for you. Call the district superintendent, and he will provide you with a candidate you either accept or reject. If you reject that candidate, the superintendent will provide another candidate, then another and so on.

Helping or Controlling?

Most denominations are set up to be of assistance to you. That's what they are there for, and theirs is a service due your church if you have sent in funds to support denominational programs and goals. Do your best to involve them in assisting you and push them some if they seem unresponsive. Conversely, some denominations may give you more help than you want by trying to control the search process for their own purposes, so watch out for that.

For example:

A Nazarene church located near a major military installation in California had grown rapidly and put up a large new sanctuary, complete with a heavy debt load. The well-regarded pastor who led them to this stage moved on, and a search committee was formed to find a new leader. The committee called the district superintendent who recommended one candidate, a fine young pastor with experience only with a smaller congregation in a growing, stable community. The committee viewed the recommended candidate rather uncritically, never sought to see a second candidate and hired him.

About the time the new pastor began his new ministry, government funding of the military complex was drastically cut and people left the area in large numbers, seriously reducing the church's income. Cutting costs, trimming church staff and struggling with tough finances was not something this pastor could handle. He resigned in his second year because "his wife's health was not able to handle the cold weather." However real that reason was, he

"Pssst . . . search committee. Back row."

Source: *Leadership,* Spring 1988, p. 23. Reprinted by permission of Rob Suggs.

retreated to an assistant pastor role in a warmer area. A more astute search committee that demanded more candidates from the district superintendent might have spared the church both this problem and the subsequent need to do a better search the next time.

Whose Responsibility?

Whether your denomination genuinely wants to help you or to control you, your search committee has the responsibility to do a good search. Since the responsibility is not anyone's except yours, don't settle for a passive, wimpy role. With some energy, creativity and persistence, the results of the search will be much better, I can assure you.

Lest I sound antidenominational, let me add a thought or two. All denominations have an understandable interest in ensuring that their pulpits are filled with competent ministers who fit within the doctrinal guidelines of the group and who support denominational goals. That responsibility alone explains why they insist on approving any candidate the congregation desires.

Also, denominations have legal and financial considerations that must be considered. In return for the funds they receive from the local church and because of the control they necessarily must exercise, it makes sense that they should help you by providing candidates with their equivalent of the Good Housekeeping Seal of Approval. Yet, if you desire to do the best possible job, you may need to test just how much freedom your own denomination will allow you.

When the denominational system is well-tuned and you have an attentive resource person at headquarters who understands the needs of your congregation, denominational involvement comes as a gift from God. When the system malfunctions, is restrictive or inept and bureaucrats don't seem to care, such involvement can seem to be the creation of Satan himself. At this point, your spiritual nature needs to be tempered by practical experience.

If you somehow believe that your denomination is the infallible and chosen servant of God and whose recommendation is a divine message, you may be in a dangerous posture. Just do some checking of the results of 10 or so referrals made to congregations that were done two or more years ago by your denominational executive. I predict you will find some referrals worked out well, some went bad and most were "okay." If so, that strongly suggests that God's leading seems to be more reliable where the search committee works hard and is assisted by able, helpful denominational support.

Of course, search committees serving independent churches or ministries have unlimited freedom in their choices. With that freedom, however, is unlimited opportunity to lay an egg, because there is no level of review or counsel to provide support. Nor is there a centralized system in place that can provide 100 dossiers of qualified candidates to help you get started. In such situations, you will probably find God's leading coming through a combination of hard work, wisdom born of prayer and a balanced practical/spiritual perspective.

If you need someone with special talents and gifts to lead your church, the likelihood is that this person is now using them successfully somewhere else. Reach out and seek such candidates through all possible means.

Passive vs. Active

The passive search committee is content to work with the candidates that come easily to them. Poor leadership and a lack of energy and vision may explain their passivity. Rev. Bill Weber, who led a Dallas "megachurch" Baptist congregation, says, "Ignorance and laziness are never blessed, no matter how well they are dedicated to the Lord."[1] I encourage you to be part of a "pro-active" committee, not a passive one.

Your results are sure to be better if you reach out with energy and imagination to find candidates that *you* feel fit your needs. If you need someone with special talents and gifts to lead your church, the likelihood is that this person is now using them successfully somewhere else. He may not have his file at denominational headquarters or be anxious to get out of his present place of ministry. Nevertheless, reach out and seek such candidates through all possible means.

Networking

"Networking" means to spread the word through all possible kinds of contacts. The term is usually used in connection with a person looking for a new position, but it also fits the situation of a search committee looking for a new leader. Who should you include in your network of sources to help you in your search? Use as many sources as you can that are likely to be helpful and to have knowledge of candidates who meet your need and who can really understand what is involved in leading your organization or congregation.

Try to avoid well-meaning people who do not have the background to know the demands of leadership or how career patterns develop. My experience suggests that every person you contact will have a name for you, but the nonprofessional isn't likely to have a productive name to suggest for a college presidency. Neither is the average person in the pew as likely to have a promising candidate for your needed pastor as a source at a seminary, Bible school or denominational headquarters. You will quickly find that a lot of time is wasted listening to useless recommendations from the well-intentioned but uninformed. Your need to be productive will probably teach you early on not to solicit this type of source.

> In all of the searches I have done for presidents of parachurch groups, someone has brought up the names of Chuck Colson and Leighton Ford as candidates. Their prominence brings to mind their leadership skills, and a board member or a staff person in even a small, rather local ministry wistfully can hope that the Lord will miraculously show these men that they should now join their group. We too often use prayer as a tool to reach unachievable goals. The unanswered prayers that result are not a reflection of God's lack of concern but evidence of our poor

understanding of the purpose and nature of prayer.

So who are the people who are well informed and are likely to be productive sources to include in your network?

Denominational headquarters. If you are denominationally connected, someone at headquarters will help you at this time. Some denominations will tell you they are the *only* source you can use. Such self-importance is not to be taken seriously.

Be sure to get from the denominational people an idea of the supply/demand ratio. If your denomination has, say, 50 open pulpits among the 500 churches and 250 dossiers are on file, you have a better idea of how selective you can be.

Seminaries and Bible schools. Whether you are independent or in a denomination, your church has a leaning toward or close involvement with one or more institutions that train church leaders. Ask each for some help from its Placement Office. They are usually better at suggesting young, recent graduates than mid-career alumni. Too, recent graduates are not as "young" as they once were and should be looked at in a new light.

Dr. Robert Cooley, president of Gordon-Conwell Seminary near Boston, says: "There is a graying of today's seminary student population."[2] Many graduates are second-career people with families and have a couple of kids each. Gordon-Conwell formerly had an average student age of 24, but now it is 32. These older graduates have a much lower failure rate than yesteryear's younger grads whose failure rate was near the 50 percent level.

Associations. Your group may be a member of or close to one of the many Christian associations that exist aside from the denominations. If you seek a leader with a foreign missions background, try any of the many independent missions boards or the International Foreign Missions Association or the Evangelical Foreign Missions Association. If you need a person to head fund-raising endeavors, ask the Christian Stewardship Council or the Evangelical Council for Financial Accountability. In religious broadcasting, your source would be the National Religious Broadcasting Association. To run your church camp, call Christian Camping International, and for administrative talent call

Christian Ministries Management Association. Separate organizations exist for Christian schools, colleges, Bible schools and many, many more.

Other leaders. Pastors talk to other pastors, college presidents talk a lot to their counterparts and so do parachurch leaders. They learn from each other, compare achievements, share frustrations and like to stay aware of what is going on in their larger world. Those factors mean they are potential sources and, on occasion, could even be possible candidates.

The itinerants. People in certain walks of life get to move from organization to organization or from congregation to congregation. As part of their vocation, they get to see more groups in action than do most people and they interact with the leaders. If you can get such a person to be in your network, you may have a unique resource. These people include all kinds of consultants, well-traveled speakers, evangelists, those who do training seminars, etc. Let your mind range widely as to who this type of person might be in your particular situation.

Placing an ad. Certain types of positions seem suitable for being advertised in print. It is normal practice for colleges to place ads in the *Chronicle of Higher Education* for professors, deans, administrators and even presidents. Such ads may look like those found on the next page.

If you are looking for an administrative person such as controller or data processing manager, an ad would fit the readership of the publication of Christian Ministries Management Association. *Christianity Today* has a section, "The Marketplace," with ads for pastors, development directors, youth directors, ministers of music, editors and comparable personnel.

The practice of running ads for a top-level leadership role is low on my list of preferred techniques, but I must include it for the sake of completeness. Its value seems greater at lower levels and when other measures are not successful. Remember, if you use ads, almost anyone can look good on paper. The best comment I've heard on this point was by Dr. Peter Drucker, the prominent management authority. He said, "As long as people write resumes, the American novel will not die."[3]

Other search committees. If your organization has a leadership

Chaplain/Director of Church Relations

ELMHURST COLLEGE

Elmhurst College, founded in 1871 by the Evangelical Synod, seeks an ordained United Church of Christ minister as Chaplain and Director of Church Relations. As Chaplain, reports directly to the President; for Church Relations to the Director of Development and Public Relations. Equal division of time between on-campus ministry and church constituency-directed activities. Salary is competitive; parsonage provided; retirement plan; tuition remission; other benefits. Located in western Chicago suburb of Elmhurst, Illinois. Send inquiry letter and background information by March 1, 1988 to: Ken Bartels, Search Coordinator, Director of Development and Public Relations, Elmhurst College, 190 Prospect Avenue, Elmhurst, Illinois 60126.

Elmhurst College is an Equal Opportunity Employer

Vice President and Treasurer

ST. OLAF COLLEGE

St. Olaf College, a distinguished liberal arts institution of the Evangelical Lutheran Church in America, seeks a strong individual to serve as its chief financial officer. The Vice President and Treasurer is responsible for the business operations of the College, including the wise management of its assets, and must be able to oversee accounting, investments, physical plant, budgeting, and payroll functions. In addition, the Vice President and Treasurer must be a creative thinker, an effective manager, and a skilled financial planner, and must be able to participate in the overall leadership of the Institution both internally and externally.

Nominations and applications should be sent by February 19. Applications should include a curriculum vitae and names of several references, and should be sent to:

Office of the President
St. Olaf College
Northfield, Minnesota 55057

An Equal Opportunity,
Affirmative Action Employer

Source: The Chronicle of Higher Education, January 27, 1988

need of a certain kind, it is certain that so has some other group rather like you in the past several years. With some research, you can probably find several such recent searches that were successfully concluded. You ought to be able to find out who chaired that search committee and, if you can build a bridge of common interest, perhaps that person will be of assistance to your committee. That committee selected the best person for *their* needs that they could attract. You may be able to attract someone they could not, and your needs are at least a little different so you may prefer someone they did not pursue very hard.

That chairman of the earlier search committee has ethical obligations and confidentiality considerations, so probe gently when you ask for help. The further back their search was completed, the less useful to you their potential help will be, but you may find real help from this source. And you will quickly realize how much time can be saved if such a source warns you away from a prospective candidate who glitters from afar but fades on closer scrutiny.

How to Approach a Source
There are three ways to approach sources: Call them, write them or see them. You have to decide what is best for your situation in view of the relationship you have with each source.

Getting access to prominent leaders is tough because their schedules are so hectic, that they must screen out matters that are of marginal value to their own tasks. Unless you know them personally, don't expect a response to the phone message you left or the letter you wrote to people such as Dr. James Dobson, Dr. Jerry Falwell, Dr. Chuck Swindoll, Dr. Billy Graham or Dr. David Hubbard. The best sources are those who have some basis for caring about you and your group in a specific way. If you graduated from Dallas Seminary and you think Dr. Howard Hendricks will remember when you were his student, go for it and call him. Or if you are a significant donor to Bethel Seminary, remind them as you lean on them a little. Don't hesitate to pick up any IOUs your committee members have outstanding.

If you don't have a good write-up of your leadership need,

shame on you and don't write to anyone. Assuming you do, follow the suggested procedure for contacting an unfamiliar source:

- Call them first and explain the need only in sketchy terms.
- Ask if you can send them your written material and then call back after they have had a chance to read it. If they don't want to cooperate, you save yourself some effort.
- *Don't* try to get suggestions of possible candidates on a first contact before they really know your need. It makes your committee look inept.
- During your call-back, as you conclude your questions, see if your source has other sources to suggest that could be helpful. If so, can you use his or her name when you call that person?
- If you know rather well a particular source that looks promising, a personal visit can be your best move.
- Every source has done you a favor, even if the person they suggested proved to be a klutz, so be sure they get your feedback later expressing your thanks and informing them how the search turned out. They probably did the best they could for you, so they warrant this courtesy.

How Many Is Enough?
Your committee probably agreed early in its discussions that the goal was to have either two, three or four well-qualified candidates to consider. Given that target, you need enough candidates to look over to yield that number. While that number may be sacrosanct, the variable that shifts may be in how "well qualified" those two, three or four are. You may find that your standards were too high for what you have to offer and so you adjust accordingly. Or, maybe as you start interviewing live candidates you realize that some things you wanted weren't important after all.

If you are blessed with more than your stated goal of two, three or four good candidates, narrow things down so that you can concentrate your attention on only the few most-promising candidates. Now you are ready to do in-depth evaluations, an interesting process that will lead you to *the* candidate.

I strongly recommend that your search committee present

only one candidate to the congregation or board. More than one usually results in divided opinions, confusion and recriminations later. Go with your best candidate, and if that doesn't work, come back with your second candidate, whom you have retained in an "in the wings" waiting status.

Do Some Checking Before You Call

Someone has given you a name of a possible candidate for your open pulpit. The endorsement is glowing and your interest quickly grows. Should you contact him? Not yet! If you call before you have some needed facts, you can get into an embarrassing situation.

In our eagerness to find "God's man" to fit our need we sometimes look at a name suggested by a respected spiritual leader as if it were almost divinely inspired truth. Sure that we are following God's leading, we eagerly place a call to the highly touted person and then realize that our emotions overruled our good judgment when it turns out that the person is unsuited or uninterested.

When you get the dossiers sent to you of people who want to be considered for the position, the problem just described doesn't develop. But when you go in "cold," you run that risk. And the impetuous, eager phone call can do just that. If the promising prospect expresses interest, but you soon discover he has a poor marriage or can't work well with his board, withdrawing from the discussions gets awkward and you fervently wish you had never called.

Seek candidates who are not looking to make a move, but do your homework before you initiate a contact. Find out as much as you can about matters you consider important so that you avoid getting into a difficult situation. Not only can your committee look stupid with an unwise call, but consider the poor candidate! You call and get his interest really high, then you drop him when you learn some disqualifying factor that you should have known from the beginning, such as age, a divorce, a health problem and so on. A number of ministers and other Christian leaders have complained to me about inept search committees that put them through a yo-yo experience of ups and downs.

I was chairing my church's pastoral selection committee when, at one of our meetings, a highly respected member had an urgent suggestion. "I have a strong feeling that we should consider Dr. Richard Halverson, pastor of Fourth Presbyterian in Washington, D.C., for our pulpit." Our committee member had not said, "God told me," fortunately, so we discussed whether Dr. Halverson, with a unique ministry among the nation's leaders, should be invited to consider a much smaller church, on the other side of the country, independent rather than denominational and having trouble in maintaining a pattern of growth. We decided not to bother Dr. Halverson, who went on to become the remarkable chaplain of the Senate.

Comparability

Our committee member's suggestion that we ask Dr. Halverson to candidate for our church was inappropriate because it overlooked the all-important factor of comparability. When we carefully looked at ourselves we saw that we were not comparable to Washington's Fourth Presbyterian in any way and that our yearning for a gifted pastor had made us selfish. Why should an outstanding leader in a place of great influence interrupt a vital ministry there simply to join us? Only a direct message from God to all of us on the committee—and to Dick Halverson—could have made such a call possible.

As time goes by, we hope to get wiser. Yet I confess that while serving on that same search committee, I, too, ignored comparability. That committee member who suggested Dr. Halverson for our church came out of a Presbyterian background and spoke from that orientation. I was from a nondenominational background, but no less presumptuous, when I actually contacted Dr. Paul Toms of historic Park Street Church in Boston. Even now, many years later, I feel embarrassment whenever I recall how I argued with Dr. Toms that our opportunities for serving Christ in a significant way were no less in our small community than they were there at Park Street Church. His turndown was gracious, as I remember—and very appropriate.

Don't expect divine intervention to make something fit that otherwise doesn't . . . . An elderly member said with great passion, "If he is God's man, age doesn't matter because God will extend his life and protect him."

The principle of comparability suggests the need for things to make sense, for the facts to fit a reasonable plan. That is, don't expect divine intervention to make something fit that otherwise doesn't. For example:

- Don't expect a leader of a large group to move to a small one.
- Don't expect an evangelist to be good in pastoral duties.
- Don't expect a career-long denominational person to go independent easily.
- Don't hope for a candidate to warm to the idea of accepting less income.
- Don't expect anyone to like the idea of developing his own financial support who hasn't done it previously.
- Don't expect great communicators to be competent administrators.
- Don't select a 65-year-old person to be the founding pastor.

I vividly remember a congregational discussion of a candidate who was in his 60s. An elderly member said with great passion, "If he is God's man, age doesn't matter because God will extend his life and protect him."

We expect a lot from God, don't we?

The Self-Anointed

In the secular world, it is not bad form to say openly that you want such and such a position and then to go after it. But not so in Christian circles, it seems. Somehow we find it important that a candidate wait to be asked and feel that any overture from the candidate himself is evidence of his being too self-seeking. Yet if God can direct a search committee to contact *the* candidate that should be selected, can He not also lay directly on the heart of that candidate a similar desire to serve their institution?

He can and He does. But, at the same time, we need to exercise a degree of discretion when considering the self-anointed candidate.

> The phone rang and when I picked it up the caller identified himself. Then he said, "God has told me that I am to be the next pastor of your church. You chair the selection committee, so I am calling you."
>
> I was flustered by this assault and finally responded by asking him to send us his papers. I added, "I'm sure that you would agree that if this is of God's leading the committee will come to agree with your feeling."

We didn't.

The world of Christians has more than its share of kooks and would-be leaders who are ill-equipped to lead. You will probably bump into a few, and your role is to find them out as soon as possible. The self-anointed ones will be likely to include such types, but don't dismiss them all without a careful scrutiny. Some may be trying to run away from a faltering situation, but others may be well qualified and may have been seeking your type of opportunity for years.

Being unemployed with a family to support and having few alternative career directions can cause someone to be more aggressive in exploring a situation—in the opinion of a search committee—than good form might otherwise prescribe. In such cases, wisdom compels us to look behind the aggressiveness to see if it really is inappropriate. I have found ministers and leaders of Christian organizations to be a rather unsophisticated group when it comes to job-seeking or changing. A 40-year-old businessman is typically more experienced at this sort of thing than is a 40-year-old minister or than is, perhaps, a 40-year-old member of a pastoral search committee. So don't allow a particular candidate's naivete or inexperience in the job search process to disqualify an otherwise suitable individual from consideration for that vacant leadership post your committee is working so hard to fill.

All right, now that you're ready, let's get on with the business at hand—candidate selection.

Notes

1. Bill Weber, quoted at Peter Drucker Management Seminar, La Verne, CA, October 1, 1978.
2. Robert Cooley, ibid.
3. "Drucker at Large" in "Musings of the Sage," *Reflections from the Lamp* 3 (Winter 1987): 2.

CHAPTER EIGHT
THE CANDIDATES LOOK AT YOU

WHETHER you are on a committee searching for a president of a college or for a pastor, you probably have never held either of those positions—if you are the usual committee member. Also, chances are that this is the first search committee you have served on. Such reasons help account for why you may lack a good understanding of the candidate's point of view. Anything you can do in advance to learn about their concerns, values and expectations will help enormously as you begin the face-to-face interviews that always seem too short. In the bibliography at the back of this book you will find some material to assist you in becoming familiar with the candidate's questions and concerns. If you can, seek out cooperative pastors or college presidents and question them about how they felt when they were candidates dealing with search committees like yours.

Being Both Practical and Spiritual
You may have an idea that people called to Christian service are different from you in their interests and aspirations. In some

ways that's true. Some are willing to work in really awful places for very little money. In faith missions they even do that and raise their own financial support. How remarkable! Even so, these special people are very logically concerned about providing for their families' well-being, the education of their kids, their own professional growth and their retirement. So don't expect candidates to be so spiritual that they don't have these valid concerns in such practical areas.

> I was interviewing Tom Houston in London about becoming the president of World Vision International. He was at the time chief executive of the British and Foreign Bible Society. When I turned the interview to his compensation history and expectations, he said, "I've never discussed that. I'm sure whatever they offered would be fine, if I was to be selected."
>
> I was greatly surprised, and my admiration for him grew. And he *was* selected![1]

When Candidates Say No

If your committee becomes aware of a potential candidate and decides to approach him, do be aware of the many good reasons why a candidate might say no to you out of hand. In those situations, the candidate need not respond with the usual, "Let me pray and think about it," so don't impugn the candidate's spiritual depth if he does that. Here are some of the reasons why candidates say no:

- He has less than two years in his present place of ministry.
- He has only a few years left until retirement.
- His primary gifts do not parallel your needs.
- His presence is required to complete a major program, such as a building program or a capital gifts campaign.
- A contract or other agreement, even verbal, has been made for him to remain longer in his present post.
- His children are in their last two years of high school.
- In his current ministry he is experiencing continuing bless-

ing from God, an ongoing challenge and no evidence of burnout.

- You are proposing a significant downward move in responsibilities and compensation or a move to a uniquely difficult ministry or place of service.

Dr. Ted Ward, a noted educator of those working in cross-cultural ministries, now teaches at Trinity Seminary. During his many earlier years at Michigan State University, he was regularly approached to go elsewhere. He and his wife felt that to discern God's leading in their lives, they had to prayerfully look at each new opportunity for service.

So many inquiries came his way that the matter became a stewardship problem. Lacking enough time to explore the offers and still do justice to his present position, Ted and his wife decided to consider a change during only one month a year. Interestingly, the inquiry from Trinity came on the thirtieth day of the month they had set aside for such considerations.

So what is the point of this little story? Simply this: Before accepting the Trinity Seminary offer, the Wards obviously had to decline a number of other offers made to them. Whether or not they gave reasons for saying no to the various invitations they received, do remember that the person your committee approaches has no obligation to tell you why he is declining your expression of interest.

If you do receive a turndown, resist the temptation to think less of that candidate than you had before. He may recently have gone through this whole process with another search committee, in which case he now feels confident that God wants him to stay right where he is. Possibly, if your committee had done more extensive research into the candidate's background, you would have seen that your approach was not wise and that his turndown was predictable.

No one likes to be turned down, neither the candidate nor your committee. Consequently, losing a "live one" can lead to a form of easy rationalization that attempts to cover or ease the ensuing sense of failure. Perhaps you can add your own ego-soothing self-deception to the list I have compiled over the years to help explain, in the manner of fishermen, why "the big one got away":

- "I'm sure the Lord has a better person in store for us."
- "Judging by the demands he made, I think he has too big an ego, no matter what his references say."
- "I think he would have come but his wife wasn't willing to relocate."
- "I think he strung us along just so he could have leverage with his board to get a raise."
- "If he couldn't see the potential of this ministry, he doesn't have the vision we need, so we are better off without him."

As long as we recognize these cop-outs for what they are, they are harmless enough.

Questions from the Candidates

A good interview should have give-and-take in it, a dialogue, not just an interrogation of the candidate by the search committee. The purpose is an exchange of information, with the candidate being as eager to learn about your group as you are about him. In fact, I would be concerned if a candidate, in the course of the interview, failed to try to learn as much as possible about the congregation or ministry he is considering.

The best way to facilitate the exchange of information is to invite the candidate's own questions as subjects are being considered. In this way, you can complete the information exchange as you proceed, rather than the candidate having to try and remember certain questions till near the end of the interview when the chair says, "Well now, do you have any questions for us?"

If you plan to use this dialogue system of interview, search committee members must be prepared to invite and respond to penetrating counter-questions from the candidates—questions not unlike those recommended by Douglas Scott in *Leadership,* a journal for clergy persons:

- Why am I of particular interest to you?

- What has been the most significant event in the life of this congregation since you have been a member?
- Aside from the upheaval of looking for a new pastor, what has been the most upsetting event in the life of this church?
- In your opinion, what areas of concern need to be addressed by this congregation?
- What kinds of things did your former pastor do particularly well?
- What were the circumstances surrounding your former pastor's departure?
- In what areas did you wish your former pastors had more expertise?
- What formal and informal methods of support have you used in the past to help your pastor become a better minister?
- Tell me about the governing board.
- Has the pastor's family traditionally taken an active role in this church?
- How is the pastor's compensation package determined? How frequently is it reviewed? By whom? What factors are used in determining that package? Merit or cost-of-living increases? Social Security reimbursement? Equity in the parsonage or a cash equity allowance? Continuing education, book, and automobile allowances?

Most relationships between a leader and his followers that go sour do so because of expectations that went unfulfilled. And the tragedy is that, in most cases, those expectations were never clearly expressed by the parties involved.

- How should your pastor spend his time? In the course of a week, how much time should be spent in prayer? Individual and family counseling? Visiting? With the family?
- What organizations in the congregation are the most active or successful?

- Beyond calling a pastor and its related concerns, what is the highest congregational priority for the next twelve months?
- What goals have you established for church growth? What methods can be used to achieve those goals?
- What plans have you made for the expansion of staff or plant?
- How stable is this congregation financially?
- What programs have you planned to implement in the next ten years?[2]

That is a great list of questions and the answers will tell your candidate about your organization. As we now know, most relationships between a leader and his followers that go sour do so because of expectations that went unfulfilled. And the tragedy is that, in most cases, those expectations were never clearly expressed by the parties involved. Careful exploration before the hiring takes place can usually avoid the disastrous results of a failed relationship.

Reactions of the Candidates

During a search process you will turn down most of the candidates, but some—as we have noted—will turn *you* down. When they do, it can make you wonder if your committee did as well as it might have. So some feedback from candidates who faced various search committees will help your committee prepare better and be more skilled at approaching candidates.

Toward this end, I conducted a survey of 50 senior pastors, heads of parachurch organizations and Christian educational institutions to get their personal reactions to the search committees that have contacted them over the years. You will find their reactions of interest and they will help prepare you to understand better the candidate's viewpoint.

Their frustrations with search committees

Spiritual arrogance by a search committee also can be viewed as the "hard sell" approach and is offensive under either name. Rev. Tom Erickson, pastor of Valley Presbyterian Church in Scottsdale, Arizona, provides an example:

Two men showed up in church one day, asked to see me following the service and informed me that God had sent them and that I was to be their new pastor. When I told them as politely as I could that I had no such communication from God, they suggested that I at least fly to their city, meet with the committee and talk further about the opportunity. Since I had had a preaching mission in that church a few years earlier, I felt I already knew all I needed to know about the church and respectfully declined.[3]

Erickson's pet peeve about search committees concerns "the lack of communication that sometimes attends the process." He expects "at least to receive an acknowledgment," when he sends in his dossier at the request of a search committee. He adds, "A prominent church in the East asked for a dossier from a good friend about five months ago. He sent it immediately and has not heard a single word from the committee since then. He wonders if he should call or write."

This sin of ignoring of a candidate who has been contacted by a committee is the most commonly noted sin of search committees.

Rev. Donald J. Kouwe, a Baptist minister who pastored for over 25 years in Indianapolis, dealt with numerous search committees over the years. He emphasizes the need for honesty by the search committee so that a sense of trust is established. The "selling" attitude of the committee can lead them to gloss over serious problems or "skeletons" in the church closet. He says, "If the committee isn't honest with you, neither will the church be later."

Kouwe is also annoyed with committees that try to be hyperspiritual or that attempt to use trick questions. Further, he disdains "association" questions, such as "What do you think of Billy Graham?" or some other leader, which are devised to place the candidate somewhere on the committee's acceptability scale.

I love this next story about the matter of compensation that a search committee raised with Kouwe. Several questions had been poorly framed to get him to state his salary requirements.

Earlier in the interview he had already decided he had no interest in the position, and he was ready when they said, "How can you determine your salary needs?"

He looked at the committee members, which included a doctor and lawyer, and said, "Why don't you each anonymously put your salary on a slip of paper in the center of the table. We'll find the average of them and I'm sure that amount will be satisfactory."

Dr. Richard Leon is senior pastor of Bellevue Presbyterian Church, Bellevue, Washington. He shares a warning to search committees that should be heeded: "Some pastors will string a committee along because of the ego feelings it generates."

His counsel to search committees is excellent when he says: "Look for the pastors who aren't looking. Don't consider only those whose dossiers come to you [from the denomination]." And, he adds, "Don't take the initial no for the final answer."

Dr. Leon also feels that committee members should visit both in the home of a candidate and in his community to see how their candidate is regarded. "God's will can be done only with openness on both sides. The better we know each other, the better the result will be," he advises.

Dr. David McKenna is president of Asbury Seminary and previously led Seattle Pacific University. He feels that "there is too much board expectation that the candidate should bring the vision for the organization with him." He has also seen a regrettable tendency for selection committees to have a denominational preference which remains unspoken during the selection process. He adds that in some cases an "outsider" is selected but then "every time a problem arises they lament, 'He doesn't understand our traditions.'"

Here are some quotes from respondents to our survey concerning their pet peeves.

"If a committee seems coy, I won't deal with them."

"Most committees won't spend the money to have the members come and visit you."

"Committees tend to be attracted to big-name preachers—who usually aren't the best pastors."

"When the committee calls the senior pastor for references, we are usually less than open because committees won't keep a confidence."

"I won't consider a church where the growth plans seem too optimistic."

"Very few committees understand what is important to a pastor."

"I refuse to fill out an 8- or 9-page form."

"If a church relies only on help from their denomination in their search, they may be poorly served."

"Don't use a seminary professor as a consultant for the search committee. They are usually out-of-touch."

"My pet peeve is when the search committee takes on more authority or responsibility than they were given."

"Some search committees try to be manipulative or get controlled by one person who tries to get his or her candidate in. It becomes a real power struggle."

"I get frustrated when search committees do not have a clear understanding of their purpose or task."

"A real protest of mine concerns any situation where politics is chosen over the leading of the Holy Spirit."

"When negotiations are entering the final stages, my experience has been that the committee decides in advance what kind of tour of the community to take the candidate on. It may, or may not, fit the interests of the candidate and family."

"When a letter comes to me asking that I fill out a form for them, but it isn't even individually addressed, I toss it. They haven't done their homework and I'm just part of a mass mailing."

Most of the survey respondents had dealt with 10 to 20 search committees over the years. Sadly, most of them rated the committees more to the "inept" side of the scale than to the "competent" side.

Their recommendations to search committees
Moving from peevishness to sagacious counsel, the respondents also shared some of the best things they have seen search committees do and made some recommendations.

Avoid the perils for the candidate that are created after a candidate accepted the offered position. Not only is it important to have the agreements with the organization clearly understood, but it is best to have them in writing.

Dr. Clyde Cook, president of Biola University, admires the creativity shown by Fuller Theological Seminary as they sought a provost when "There was really a paradigm shift in thinking to suggest that perhaps a board member who was a successful surgeon could make a good provost. Ask yourself questions that are not always expected." I suspect Dr. Cook admires the daring but spirit-led selections some years ago when committees at Fuller chose a 32-year-old David A. Hubbard as seminary president and at Boston's historic Park Street Church when they selected Harold John Ockenga, then also a very young man, as their minister.

Dr. Ed Stephens, the president of George Fox College, in

Newbury, Oregon, was impressed by the way their search committee did its work. They had all candidates tape their responses to a list of questions with which they had been supplied. The tapes were shared with board members.

His counsel for search committees is:

1. Select a well-organized chairperson and provide him the needed support services to do the job.
2. When planning the schedule of candidates' interviews, don't have too many or have them close together. Allow some personal time.

Rev. Garth Bolinder, senior pastor of Hillcrest Covenant church in Prairie Village, Kansas, adds to that last thought. "It is most helpful to candidates when a search committee provides some rest and reflection time during the busy interview process. During our last candidating session, we were able to stay in a very nice hotel. This gave us some much-appreciated down-time in which to rest and reflect upon the impact of the interview process. We were also invited to stay at that hotel on the first night we arrived in the new city after our move. It provided a sense of congruence and a welcome."

He counsels search committees to avoid the perils for the candidate "that are created after a candidate accepts the offered position. He or she now no longer relates to the search committee, who may have painted rather glowing terms and conditions about the job, situations and organization. Now the candidate relates to a different group of people, the church board, and the candidate finds that the rules have changed and that some of the agreements no longer apply. Not only is it important to have the agreements with the organization clearly understood, but it is best to have them in writing."[4] Let me add, it is not only "best" to have things in writing, it is *essential*.

Rev. Tom Erickson has another experience to share with you:

During the lunch I was impressed by the spontaneous way in which the members of the committee kept changing chairs so they could all be near Carol [Mrs. Erickson] and have an opportunity to engage her in conversation. It was obvious that they were deeply interested in her viewpoints and wanted her to feel comfortable with them. The moral is that committees should show as much care for the spouse and family as they do for the candidate. The spouse is not being called or employed, but the success of the pastor is inextricably bound up with the comfort and security of the family.

Rev. Vic Pentz, a pastor in Yakima, Washington, chaired the 1987 presidential search committee at Whitworth College. He feels one of the better things the members did "was to balance goal-oriented activities with prayer and personal involvement. When the chips were down, disappointments came and tempers flared, our personal affection and mutual trust in the Lord were all that held us together. Our meetings began with a brief devotional and all closed with conversational prayer."

Dr. David McKenna, head of Asbury Seminary, makes this observation: "Times of transition are a golden opportunity to step back and see where the institution has been, is now and is going over the next five years. A search committee who handles this task well becomes very credible and persuasive."

Another source emphasizes the importance of selecting well the chair of the search committee: "You should never get a chairperson by default. For a year or more this responsibility will need to be the dominant thing in this person's life."

- I conclude here with two humorous comments from the survey: Know where you are going when you go to see a candidate. Sioux Falls, South Dakota is not the same as Sioux City, Iowa. The committee chairman was quite late for our meeting, even though he was flying his own plane.

- You should be sure that where you meet is suitable for the interview. When we got to the hotel, the dining room was closed, so we were put in the cocktail lounge. In the next booth was a fellow loudly telling off-color stories. As the food was served, I asked the blessing very loudly and [the fellow] stopped. The interview certainly wasn't what it could have been.

Notes
1. Quotation and personal information are used by permission of Tom Houston.
2. Douglas G. Scott, "Getting the Real Story: A Guide to Candidating," *Leadership* (Summer 1984), pp. 24-29. Used by permission.
3. All responses to the author's survey that are quoted in this chapter are published with the respondents' permission.
4. Garth assures me that his comments here are not based on his experiences with or the actions of the Hillcrest Covenant Church search committee.

CHAPTER NINE

EVALUATING THE CANDIDATES

CHAIRMAN: "We now have 54 candidates whose papers have been sent to us by our denominational offices. Also, five more have come to us from people who heard of our need and there are three more I know who are outstanding whom I would like to go after. I would assume some of you committee members may also have ministers in mind you would like us to consider."

Committee member: "In preparation for this meeting, I briefly scanned the files we have received. While a few of them don't meet our criteria, a lot of them seem to and have outstanding backgrounds. How on earth are we going to be able to sift through them all to find our new pastor?"

Sifting the wheat from the chaff—that's the necessary problem the search committee faces at this point. You have worked hard to get this large number of prospective candidates, mostly well-qualified ones, and now comes the tough process of selectively dismissing all of them but one.

You probably are excited at the possibility of finding God's man for your church among the candidates, but you cringe at the idea of telling so many people that you do not find them acceptable for your pulpit. If that's the way you feel, it is very understandable. Every sensitive person would. With that assurance, move bravely on to find that one special candidate who best fits your needs.

The Rough Cut
From the job description you prepared, you can easily devise a list of criteria that lets you sort through the candidates and dismiss those who don't come close to meeting your needs. Location, education, an unstable work history, inappropriate experience, making too much money now, and so on—a variety of reasons will tell you whom to dismiss first. This rough cut will reduce the pile of papers somewhat, but probably not a lot.

Further Winnowing
The next cut takes more work. You may want to develop your own rating scale to help, and it is discussed a few pages on. At this point, you will probably start doing some telephone reference-checking and calling some candidates to get details that interest you, but aren't in the papers you have.

The Finalists
All of this evaluating and sifting should lead you to the most promising three, four or five candidates of the bunch—on paper—perhaps even one or two more. These warrant your getting to know them in greater depth and seeing if there is a good response from them to your opening. To do this usually involves correspondence, phone calls, reference-checking and perhaps listening to each one preach without his knowing you are there.

From this increased scrutiny you should be able to have two or three candidates who are of the greatest interest to you and who seem genuinely interested in your church. These are your finalists. You will want to have them interviewed by the search committee as the final screening/evaluating step in the long search process.

"Then it's passed by a 3-2 vote that from now on
we'll announce all decisions as unanimous."

Source: *Leadership*, Fall 1984, p. 35. Reprinted by permission of Erik D. Johnson.

Be cautious though. Don't sign off the next best two or three candidates until you are sure things are progressing nicely with your preferred finalists.

Planning the Interview

The group interview is the accepted standard way to get to know a candidate personally. In it, the entire search committee meets with the candidate, questions him and responds to his queries about the college, church or parachurch organization. The primary advantage of the group interview is that the whole committee shares a common experience as they watch the candidate react and respond.

An interview with just two or three people can probably be more effective; it is less imposing and formal so reactions can be more spontaneous and less guarded. However, if the small group perceives something they feel is significant that does not reveal itself in the meeting with the whole committee, the problem arises of how to convince the larger group of the validity of what they—the smaller group—experienced.

An example:

> The search committee chair said, "When just the three of us were with him he made some comments about his wife that makes me wonder about the relationship. It wasn't what he said as much as it was the way he said it, as we were talking about their housing needs."
> A member of the search committee who was at the meeting of the whole committee but not at the smaller one, responded, "Well, none of that was evident when we were with him. I can't imagine there is a problem."
> The other committee members nodded assent and the chairman realized he lacked the support of his committee to dig more deeply.

Group interviews need to be carefully planned. Specific members should have questions assigned to them and, as they focus their attention on the asking and the clarifying with follow-up questions, other members can record the candidate's response for later evaluation. The chairman is responsible for directing traffic so that no single person dominates the interview.

No one issue should cause things to bog down. For instance, if your committee desires to see where the candidate stands on the inerrancy of Scripture, it could be more efficient to advise him in advance what your position is and ask if he accepts it or differs from it in any significant way. Questions on complex issues, such as inerrancy, can generate incomplete or unclear responses that unnecessarily cause tension and misunderstanding while slowing down the interview's progress. As traffic cop, the chairman has the responsibility to keep things moving, so all the needed material is covered.

No Trick or Hypothetical Questions

An interview is not a place to sandbag a candidate or to show how clever your questions can be. "What if—" is the way most hypothetical questions start, and they often signal an attempt to put the candidate into a box from which he can escape only with the correct answer. A candidate with a good level of self-confidence will have limited patience with such contrivances.

The Interview

By the time your committee meets face-to-face with a candidate, you already know quite a bit about him through the material he has sent to you. Similarly, he should have digested all you sent to him about your church, it's history, current situation, programs and doctrinal position. You probably have also learned quite a bit about each other from inquiries you have made and now you both should have high expectations from these discussions. It is now time for that first face-to-face meeting, to see if all the preliminary work is going to pay off. You are probably going to hold this type of interview with the two or three preferred candidates, so it is important to give thought to how you should do it.

Research shows that interviews are among the least accurate methods of screening leaders and predicting their future performance. Nevertheless, we emotionally need the personal interaction of the interview, the opportunity to feel the impact of the candidate's personality. Even if we had read the research on interviewing effectiveness, we would have dismissed it because we feel the need for the face-to-face encounter. As Christians, we are inclined to ignore statistical studies because we feel that things of the Spirit are not discovered in that manner.

The Setting
Depending on what is most convenient, the interview could be held on your turf or his, or in another spot where neither side has a "home court advantage." If the candidate has only a nominal level of interest at this point, but you are pursuing him with excitement, you may have to go see him. If the candidate is highly interested, he usually will accommodate you.

Wherever you hold the interview, it must afford privacy from congregational members, telephone calls and other intrusions. The site should be comfortable, have available restrooms and provide suitable refreshments. A quite simple arrangement is to use a hotel meeting room for the interview and have the lunch served there, too. The confidentiality of your meeting can be well managed under such circumstances.

A good sequence is a morning session of two hours (9:30-11:30), a break after an hour, a lunch (12:00-1:30) and an afternoon session of up to two more hours. It may not take that long, and you could advise the candidate in advance that the time needed after lunch "will be whatever we feel the need of, but it won't last longer than four o'clock." That gives you the flexibility to do what seems best as matters proceed during the day.

The "eager beaver" candidate
A candidate who is now unemployed or under pressure to leave where he presently ministers is most likely to be this anxious-to-please type of person. It takes more patience and creativity to evaluate the eager beaver than any other type of candidate.

Usually, it is easy to tell when you have an eager beaver on your hands just from his comments, attitudes and lack of penetrating questions. Your initial task is to find out why he is so desirous to become your leader, even though genuine enthusiasm and excitement about your opportunity is a welcome quality and shouldn't be misunderstood. But if, when your questions really bore in, the candidate's eagerness seems primarily based on self-interest, the committee itself—in most cases—will lose interest. An insightful and honest candidate will often discuss the possibility of being interested for the wrong reasons and will ask for prayer or counsel in how best to weigh whether an acceptance would be for the valid reasons.

> Our candidate was presently serving a small church in Massachusetts. His youngest daughter had a physical problem that made it medically advisable to move to a warm climate and we were about to offer him the pastorate of a much larger church in sunny southern California. He shared with us, the search committee, his worry that he might allow concern over his daughter to cause him to accept our offer for the wrong reasons. From his strict Christian childhood and Wheaton College years, his built-in guilts prepared him to wonder whether anything that seemed so desirable could be in God's will. Eventually he accepted our call and had fifteen years of successful ministry with us.

Obviously, good things can and do come to us from the hand of God, even in this life. But in some cases, the search committee will need to assist the candidate in sifting his own motivations as he considers coming to join you. If he seems shallow in his analysis, he may be playing games with you or with himself. Or, he may just be a shallow person—and that you need to find out.

Your task is made more difficult because a candidate's motives can be pure but misunderstood by a pressing style or reaction in the interview. If he faced a lack of income for his family, wanted to escape an irrational board or saw a very attractive opportunity, some excessive eagerness is understandable. But that is no reason to dismiss the candidate.

Your challenge is to get through these distractions, with the candidate's help, and to find out what he is really like. One way to do that has already been suggested: Have him discuss with you the obviously attractive things about your situation and how

---

"If your search committee sets its sights on a rising star or an established leader, get ready for extra effort and anticipate the need for some genuine creativity."

---

he weighs them as he considers ministry with you. Similarly, discuss the negatives too.

If you suspect he is willing to "be all things to all people," test how far he would go with some carefully crafted queries. With some creativity you should be able to allow the eagerness of an opportunistic candidate to carry him way out to the end of a limb. If he senses his predicament of being trapped by his own doing, you may not even need to saw it off.

The "reluctant bride" candidate

"The best candidates are always the hardest to get." The corollary of that truism is that the best candidates get lots of invitations to consider new ministry opportunities and they get weary of such contacts. They learn how disruptive it is to their commitment to consider a possible change, so they find it necessary to make fairly difficult the approaches by search committees. If your search committee sets its sights on a rising star or an established leader, get ready for extra effort and anticipate the need for some genuine creativity. You surely didn't get his dossier from the denominational offices, because he isn't actively looking, so you have to make an unusually effective presentation to have any chance of success.

In chapter 8, I discuss a number of reasons why you should accept a quick turndown from a candidate with no hard feelings toward him. If your target candidate does not fit those particular categories, then press on with your effort to obtain him. After all, a Christian leader seldom has felt called to a ministry before he knew about it, so you must make the need/opportunity known.

However you can do it, find a way to get to the person you have in mind. Because of his initial lack of interest, you may have to use more time and extra effort to get his involvement. After you have seen him face-to-face and he still has given no encouragement, you have to consider letting go of him and to better use your time and energies with other candidates. Just be careful that you don't give up too soon, however.

> I was assisting the search committee of a large, diversified ministry in the Pacific Northwest in their search for a new chief executive officer. A candidate of outstanding promise came to my attention, and I traveled to Chicago to meet him. He was all I had hoped for except that his interest in our situation was counterbalanced by good reasons to stay where he was. He was interested but not enough, it seemed to me.

> The board chairman of the ministry was active on the search committee and he disagreed with my recommendation to drop this candidate because of his limited interest in us. My second and third contacts left me convinced that our candidate was very well-qualified but would never accept an offer. We looked at another excellent candidate, but the board chairman retained his conviction that our "reluctant bride" was God's man for us, much to my annoyance.
>
> The end of the story is that the board chairman's persistance resulted in the selection of his preferred candidate and a distinguished leadership is unfolding marvelously. I believe there are two morals to this story:

1. Good things—and God's will—don't always come easily or quickly, and
2. Consultants aren't as smart as they think they are. (But you already knew that, didn't you?)

The "teaser" candidate

A teaser, as you would expect, encourages you to believe he is interested but then disappoints you by withdrawing from the selection process.

Here are some of the reasons why a candidate can become a teaser:

- Indecisiveness. At the last minute, he can't bring himself to make the change.
- That "being wanted" feeling. Back home his congregation isn't offering him much affirmation, knowing all his faults. The search committee, seeing most clearly his strengths, makes him feel really wanted as they pursue him. After the flush of ego nourishment ebbs, he stays where he is, where there is less risk and no disruption of relationships. (The same pattern explains a number of extramarital affairs.)
- Is it the Lord calling? This type of candidate is so insecure in his efforts to be "where the Lord wants me" that he feels he must always be responsive to a call such as yours because it "may be God's will for my life." His desire to "be open to God's leading"—or is it an uncertainty about God's previous leading?—causes him to consider every opportunity that comes his way and creates anxiety in his wife and children.

The only way I know of to weed out teasers as early as possible is to look at the stability of their work history and to try and find out how many other churches may have unsuccessfully pursued them.

Courtesy Requirements

It's only 30 minutes into the interview with a candidate, but already you know with a sense of certainty that he *isn't* your man. How do you get out of this unpromising situation as quickly as possible without being rude? Your committee members are busy people, you realize, and they aren't inclined to act out a charade, so you want to end the interview.

My feeling is that if you find that the candidate deliberately falsified something, such as claiming a degree he didn't earn, not mentioning a divorce and the like, bring it out immediately for discussion. Gently confront the candidate with the problem and get the candidate's response. You may have misunderstood something, but if the fabrication remains a problem, ask for a recess from the interview, see what your committee wants to do and call him back for that decision. If the candidate created the problem, as in this case, you have a minimal responsibility.

However, if in your discussion you find a problem that the candidate could not have foreseen, you need to spend more time. For example, if his salary requirements come as a surprise to you and are well above what you can offer, you were probably at fault in letting things go this far without learning this fact. Similarly, if he stumbled over a cleverly concealed theological trip wire and just blew himself up in the opinion of your committee, you owe him every possible consideration and courtesy, despite your lack of continuing interest.

You, not he, initiated these discussions. He is here at your invitation, and he warrants all the privileges of an honored guest and Christian brother. Unless a falsification is involved, as discussed previously, you probably are obligated to complete the interview and the lunch. In any case, every reasonable effort should be made to make the interview a positive experience for all parties, even if it obviously will lead no further.

If the interview has gone badly, you probably cannot let the candidate know you have decided against him until your committee meets after the interview to see where things went wrong. If it can be done gracefully, let him know there are some problems that have to be discussed but, in any case, don't give him false hopes which you would shortly have to dash. Promise to be back in touch with him promptly—in two or three days—and do so, sharing with him whatever you can that would be of value to him if he is in a job search.

Interviewing the Spouse

I cannot imagine anyone being hired for a Christian ministry position without the spouse also being interviewed. However, I recommend that the spouse be invited to the second interview, not the first, where the interest is appropriately focused on the person being hired. Sometimes, however, interviewing both marriage partners at once can bring about the appearance of problems that really don't exist.

> He was an outstanding candidate for the CEO position for my client, a parachurch ministry. He was coming to the U.S.A., and my only chance to interview him was with his wife over a meal at their hotel. Late in the interview, I switched my questions to his wife but was unable to get a response from her. My fourth question to her was, "Does your husband ever allow you to answer your own questions?" Fortunately, I had correctly guessed that they both had good ego strength and a sense of humor. She then responded well to my questions and I could sense his pride in her and in her numerous accomplishments. In many marriages, one person steps on the other's lines.

The Questions to Be Asked

If the search committee reviews all the material they have on the candidate's background before going to the interview, considerable time can be saved. With the factual data as a backdrop, the challenge now is to find out what the real person is like. Your questions will hopefully provide insights into his beliefs, attitudes and value system, all of which are important.

While you are listening to his responses and evaluating them you will be developing an impression of how well he communicates and relates to others, factors which we tend to call "personality." This can sometimes result in the answer to a question being less important than how he says it. Whether or not it is wise or even fair, "personality" is what seems to be the most important part of an interview to a search committee, that is, if no serious flaws are uncovered in doctrinal areas and no glaring deficiencies surface in the experience or background of the candidate being interviewed.

We have already discussed the fact that a good interview consists of a give-and-take dialogue between committee and candidate, and we have looked at the counter-questions a serious candidate might ask of the committee. But what of the questions the committee members have prepared to ask of the candidate? Your questions, of course, should be carefully thought out in advance, so as to cover your major areas of interest. And each committee member should be prepared to ask several questions in areas of special interest to him or her.

The use of a list of questions, rather than just winging it, allows you to compare the responses of each candidate on each question, a practice which may be helpful in the postinterview evaluations by your committee. Of the numerous lists I have reviewed that various denominations have prepared for search committees, I like best the one from the Reformed Church in America (RCA). Naturally, any list you adopt will need to be altered to fit your particular needs, but the one by the RCA is a good starting place:

1. Please tell us about the ministry you are in right now.
2. As you look back, what has happened which you feel best about?
3. What in your present situation is disappointing to you?
4. If you were to stay there another five years, what would you like to see happen?
5. From what you have seen about our church, is there anything which seems particularly challenging?
6. How would you describe your methods of leadership?
7. What in the ministry do you consider to be your specialty?
8. How did you come to choose the ministry as a vocation?
9. As you look back over your life, where do you see yourself making critical choices?
10. How has your own faith and your theological views changed since you entered college? Since you entered the ministry?
11. What are your views on _____? (Choose any theological or social issues which are important in your congregation.)
12. Describe the process you go through when you are preparing a sermon.

13. What is your preferred practice with regard to pastoral calling? What is your objective, what do you do, what makes you decide to make a call?
14. What emphasis do you place on pastoral counseling? Please describe your training and experience in this area.
15. What role does your family play in your practice of ministry?
16. What issues do you see as the most important ones facing our denomination right now?
17. How do you understand the role of the minister in church administration?
18. What approaches to a congregation's financial stewardship do you prefer?
19. If you were to become the pastor of this church, what are some of the things you would try to do during your first year here?
20. How do you maintain your own spiritual, emotional, and physical health?
21. (Add questions
22. your committee
23. decides are
24. particularly important.)[1]

The Baptist General Conference has some excellent questions that the RCA list does not cover:

1. How do you prefer to work with a Deacon Board?
2. Would you share your practice or habits in allocation of time including preservation of personal/family time.
3. What title do you prefer?
4. What is your attitude toward Christians of other denominations?
5. What feelings, needs, expectations do you have about paid staff?
6. How much involvement do you want personally in the community?
7. What opportunities do you see at our church and how do they fit with your interests and gifts?[2]

The Cumberland Presbyterian Church denomination has a different list, from which I have selected these:

1. How do you determine what priorities to put on tasks you must do?
2. Would you care to share any of your weaknesses with us?
3. What are your future plans for continued personal and professional growth?
4. How do you like to spend your free time?[3]

In my interviewing, I usually ask about the successes and failures the candidate has experienced. Often I begin my questioning with this invitation, "Would you please tell me about your faith pilgrimage and where it has brought you?" A commonly used closing question is, "After all of this, what have we left out that we should have covered?"

An arbitrary and capricious board can use (termination) unjustly as a weapon, while a thoughtful and wise board may use it in a proper fashion.

"But He Was Fired from His Last Place—"

The inference was plain that the search committee member speaking was not willing to consider the person they were discussing. The committee members looked down at the resume, fidgeted a little and were quiet until the chairman said, "Let's move on to the next candidate."

I would wish for you greater wisdom than that committee had. Many fine candidates for leadership have been fired along the way and are now better candidates because of it. And what is a firing anyway? An involuntary termination, no more or no less. An arbitrary and capricious board can use it unjustly as a weapon, while a thoughtful and wise board may use it in a proper fashion. My point is that, in any firing, the burden of proof should be no more on the candidate than on the board that fired him. In my experience, I see more faults to be laid to the charge of boards than to the discharged persons.

More commonly than not a resignation is the reason for the ending of a relationship. As a search committee, you need to know whether the resignation was voluntary, suggested or requested. Genteel Christian folks try to avoid a public fracas, so "resignation" often really means "resign, so that we won't have to fire you." Some leaders under fire believe they are standing on important principle and demand to be fired to make a point.

As a search committee, you need to consider a candidate who resigned as being just the same as one who was fired. There may be no difference.

Dr. Peter F. Drucker says, "No significant achiever makes it without a failure before 40."[4] He said this to a group of Christian leaders, not to business executives, and there is wisdom in his counsel, as usual. Such failures sometimes get a leader fired. Your job is to see if the failure/firing has caused the candidate to grow or to retreat and rationalize.

Roy C. Price, in his article, "When the Pastor Gets Fired," makes some excellent points about how deeply getting fired impacts the individual. "Since God has chosen to use adversity to produce maturity and character in those he calls, being fired can yield good fruit. One pastor clarified his desire to be in a country church. Another said his devotional life increased as he grew closer to God and to his wife—the only ones he had to talk with.

"A third said that after it was over, he had come to feel a lot better about himself, discovering an area he needed to change. 'I need to learn to be more objective about my ideas. When I feel I'm not being heard or am feeling threatened, my voice lowers and I come across as angry. It appears I've lost my cool. I can see that in the discipline of my child as well.' To a fourth, his experiences led him to a new understanding of death to self, and living in the power of the Holy Spirit.

"Each of them said firing gave greater sensitivity to others' suffering. As a result, each sought to extend love and encouragement. 'I needed someone to reassure me that I was OK, that God loved me and I wasn't a failure. I had no one—so now I try to do that for others. The period of struggle can have a happy ending. The Devil's temptation is to doubt God and seek revenge. We must be honest before God and go on."[5]

A search committee is usually an intimidating group to a candidate, particularly to one who has been fired. Such a person finds it hard to feel secure enough with the committee to allow a discussion of the firing, so it is an unusual committee that can create the openness to allow it.

It is also a rare search committee that even will consider such a candidate, if they know about the firing when they are reviewing candidate files early in the search. That is one reason why a candidate will try to avoid saying he was fired. Committees that engage in such early, easy dismissals have a play-it-safe attitude that may deny them a choice servant of God who is growing into significant ministry. Also, it is unfair to candidates who have invested so much of themselves to deny them the opportunity to shepherd a flock.

If your group has theological tenets, life-style considerations or a basis of fellowship that you suspect could be a problem for the candidate, tell him where you stand and why and then invite his reaction. Seeking to get a candidate to say something that is self-incriminating so you can dismiss him is unkind, very inefficient and a poor reflection on the committee's intent and abilities.

Be sure to remember that a break is probably appropriate after about one hour. You may feel things have hardly warmed up after the first hour, but consider how much pressure the candidate is under. If he begins to sweat, seems distracted or starts to get defensive, take a break and get a fresh start.

Be sure to recall that right after lunch—even the light one you thoughtfully ordered—things tend to slow a bit. And then there is the maxim of educators: "The head cannot absorb more than the seat can endure."

Rating the Candidates
When you are looking at the credentials of a number of qualified

candidates, the process of deciding whom to focus your attention on and whom to make "finalists" can get confusing. Even worse, the personal preferences of the committee members make it difficult to weigh the various factors unemotionally. Here are comments such as you might hear in your committee discussions:

> "Rev. Jones has spent his whole life in the south. Do you think he and his family could adjust to our Midwest way of life?"
> "Rev. Smithson had five years in business before going to seminary, and I like some 'real world' experience in my pastor."
> "My sister lives in Rev. Matthews' town and has heard him preach. She says he has a marvelous voice and is very good looking."
> "Rev. Brenner has a higher salary requirement than we want to pay but he more than meets all our requirements—and his wife works. Should we go for him?"

Money, regional differences, educational background, family structure, preaching style, appearance and voice—the variables at times seem endless. Any aid that you can devise to evaluate better these factors is a rating scale (see the sample form in this chapter). It will help your committee members clarify their thoughts and help them arrive at the needed decisions.

People, such as accountants and engineers, who like to quantify things find these devices most helpful. And rating scales do not take long to build, unless you have a divided committee. Even then, the committee chairman will find rating scales helpful in leveling out the excessive influence of an aggressive committee member or the overriding impact of a single concern about a candidate that seems to overshadow everything else.

Using the position description that you prepared earlier, list all the factors you feel will be important in making your decision. Initially, this list will include everything that has come up as you have sorted through the backgrounds of the candidates. As your committee makes the list, what will become obvious to all is that some factors are vital while a few seem trivial. Realizing that fact leads you very logically to the weighing of the factors.

Weighting the Factors

Of all the factors you have listed, some are of a "must" nature. All your candidates *must* meet these criteria to warrant your further consideration. Such items would surely include your educational requirements, ordination, denominational affiliation and doctrinal beliefs. There probably won't be many "must" factors.

The weighting of the remaining items is the assigning of the relative importance of each. If your most important factor is estimated to be three times as valued as your least important, use a 1 to 3 scale. Or you could use a 1 to 4 or a 1 to 5, as seems best to you. If 3 is your highest/best score, you may feel that the factor "preaching" is worth a 3 but "visitation" is only a 2 in your church. Your committee should be able to do this weighting of each factor without much fuss.

I promise this won't get complicated, so don't stop until you take the next step with me.

With all your factors weighted, you are now ready to rate your candidates as fairly as you can. Your rating scale will be your tool for adding up the perceived strengths and weaknesses of each candidate and making useful comparisons. People seem to like a 1 to 5 (5 is high) scale for rating each weighted factor for each candidate.

Be sure each committee member puts in the weighting of each factor correctly before they do the rating of the candidates. The higher the score the candidate gets, the greater his apparent acceptability to the committee. (You may have to remind any golfer on the committee that to be the lowest is *not* best.)

A warning: Rating scales can be helpful as a tool in reducing the number of candidates or even in working with the finalists, but don't take them too seriously. They are not "truth," only process tools to help the members see how opinions of the candidates are developing. A growing feeling of consensus is needed for a committee to move well to a satisfactory conclusion.

CANDIDATE RATING SCALES

Factors	Weighting (1 to 3)	Individual Ratings (1 to 5)		
		BERHOLZ	GATES	REHNBERG
Appearance	x1	5	4	3
Voice	x1	3	3	4
Preaching	x2	6	8	10
Personality	x3	9	12	15
Education	x1	4	3	4
Board Relationships	x2	8	6	8
Experience	x3	6	9	6
Community Involvement	x1	1	3	4
Family	x2	4	8	10
TOTAL		46	56	64

If the results of the rating scales show a lack of agreement, the chairman needs to get creative and find ways to break the deadlock. In most cases, it would be unfortunate, I believe, to have an agreement in advance that the rating scale results would be the final basis for retaining or dropping a candidate. While their use can be helpful, there are statistical and emotional reasons for not letting them be the last word.

Here is a final thought on rating scales. As often as not, when the face-to-face interviews are held, the impact of rating scales is lost because the committee develops a strong feeling of preference for a particular candidate. The numbers and the logic of the ratings lose their persuasiveness when the feeling of warmth and mutual acceptance develops and is interpreted by the committee as meaning he is God's man for their ministry. When the candidate responds similarly, this is usually seen as a confirmation of the leading of God. With the earlier use of rating scales, I feel fairly confident that your finalists were well qualified and you are now well positioned to move as you feel led.

One Candidate, Not More

It is important, I believe, for the search committee to present only one candidate at a time to the board and/or congregation. Every author I've read or denominational handbook I have seen agrees with the one-at-a-time policy. Why? There are a number of good reasons and few of merit for having more.

First, as the authorized committee of the church or board, the search committee has the responsibility to make the decision, subject to the approval of the authorizing body. With more than one candidate, the weight of the search committee's full endorsement is absent.

Second, with presenting a second candidate at the same time, you are creating the necessity for having a "loser," because you will hire only one. I also suspect most candidates would have difficulty with being presented as one of two choices. They know how difficult it is for an individual to come to you as a candidate and preach at your church while keeping the matter confidential from his current congregation. With that problem exacerbated by only a 50 percent chance of being selected, why run the risk?

Third, the most important reason is that the congregation— or the whole board—are not as well qualified to vote on the candidates as you are. Having only listened to a single sermon or having held only one overly large group interview, they cannot judge as competently as can the committee which has studied and evaluated the candidate closely. Consequently, such bodies are limited to judging the candidates on the basis of such superficial factors as personality or preaching style.

Fourth, forcing a choice of multiple candidates creates a popularity contest and those who preferred the candidate who was not selected may find it difficult to be supportive of the new leader. Presenting multiple candidates assures a built-in opposition.

If one candidate gets a high plurality vote, you know your committee made a big mistake in presenting the other candidate. That candidate is humiliated by his low vote and the winner is sobered by the fact that whoever voted for the other person is not in favor of his being there.

So remember, one at a time, please!

Notes
1. "Conduct an Interview," *Handbook for Pastoral Search* (New York: Office of Human Resources, Reformed Church in America, n.d.), pp. 57-59. Used by permission.
2. "Questions for the Candidate," *Pastoral Search Committee Phone Interview Guidelines* (Arlington Heights, IL: Baptist General Conference, n.d.). Used by permission.
3. *Our Pastor Is Leaving. Now What?* (Memphis, TN: Cumberland Presbyterian Church, n.d.). Used by permission.
4. "Drucker on Leadership" in "Musings of the Sage," *Reflections from the Lamp* 3 (Winter 1984): 1.
5. Roy C. Price, "When the Pastor Gets Fired," *Leadership,* Fall 1983, p. 55. Used by permission.

CHAPTER TEN

THE FINE ART OF CHECKING REFERENCES

A major flaw in the selection process with most Christian groups is that they are usually satisfied too easily. What the search committee sees on paper and even feels from an interview with the candidate are valuable parts of the process, but they are not enough. For many committees the die is cast when the candidate gives the correct answers to the theology questions, has a good personality and a record of competence in previous positions.

If a warm glow develops toward the candidate in some of the committee members who are persuasive, the momentum starts to build. Then someone is likely to say in a stately fashion, "I believe this is God's man for us." That can settle the matter of the choice.

And it often leads to serious trouble!

I suggest that the scenario just described is sloppy work and not what a good search committee will do. To cloak a half-done task in spiritual garb is an old trick among Christians, though usually it's done unknowingly. But it does not serve us well.

Here's what I mean:

> The leader of a prominent youth ministry organization once said to me, "We selected a very promising person to head up a ministry but he didn't work out at all. I guess God didn't want him to be here."
> Without showing the degree of respect I really feel for this man, I blurted out: "Please don't blame the Lord for what you could have avoided with a few simple reference checks."

Search committees need to remember that Christian leaders who are candidating for a position—whether for that of a pastor,

---

"This tendency toward ignoring or denying the obvious results in a superficiality that makes it difficult for Christians to ask penetrating questions of Christian leaders."

---

of a parachurch organization executive or of a college president—are trained, able communicators. They also are usually well-tailored, demonstrate good social skills and have personalities that are—at least, initially—quite engaging. And naturally, theology is "their thing."

Usually then, it is "no contest" when the average committee and candidate meet. The person you seek to know may be as charming as you initially believe him to be, but you need to prove it. If that committee member is correct that "this is God's man for us," a thorough check of references will confirm that fact and, thereby, convince the whole committee. However, if that committee member is only hallowing a personal feeling, careful reference checking may save the committee from presenting a future disaster to the group they serve.

"He Looks Great, but How Can We Be Sure?"
The art of reference checking seems to hold little interest in Christian circles but is seen as mandatory in making executive

"Jimmy, we're the Pastoral Search Committee,
and we'd like to ask you a few questions about
your dad."

Source: *Leadership*, (Summer 1985), p. 36. Reprinted by permission of Doug Hall.

selections in the business world. The Alban Institute's otherwise fine booklet, *So You're on the Search Committee,* by Bunty Ketcham (24 pp.) ignores reference checking as one of the five key tasks of the search committee. The Presbyterian Church (U.S.A.) has a helpful mimeographed piece *On Calling a Pastor,* also 24 pages in length. But it also devotes only half a page to checking references.

The Christian landscape is littered with debris, both personal and organizational, due to the poor choosing of leaders. Many of the mistakes were not due to anything new that developed in the life of the person after he was selected; they were just unknown to the search committee. Similarly, the prospective leader often fails while candidating to dig deeply enough in getting references on the church or college considering him. Inevitably then, all parties concerned are unhappily surprised later on.

Why these lethal surprises? Four reasons seem to explain it.
1. Christians are particularly prone to believing the best about people, particularly of spiritual leaders.
2. Both the organization doing the search and the candidate put their best foot forward and tend to conceal their flaws and limitations.
3. Good reference checking takes time, courage and some skills to do.
4. Search committee members often have too much confidence in their ability to "read people" or to get divine messages about the candidates.

Perhaps you find these four points insulting and want to refute them. Read on before you decide, please.

Point One: The gullibility of Christians is a factor.
Christians are a redeemed people; not perfect, it's true, but redeemed. We understandably emphasize the finer, spiritual aspects of our lives and try to ignore evidences of the old nature. We largely expect other Christians not to inquire about any part of our lives that is not Christ-honoring, and we extend to them the same courtesy. But this tendency toward an operative style

of ignoring or denying the obvious results in a superficiality that makes it difficult for Christians to ask penetrating questions of Christian leaders.

I suspect another influence increases the reluctance to conduct meaningful reference checks. Matthew 7:1 says to Christians, "Judge not, that ye be not judged," and many believers apply this Scripture mistakenly. This verse actually refers to our having an unforgiving, harsh spirit in judging another person, not to our evaluating that person's suitability for holding a particular post. Thus, checking references is not prohibited by God's Word; rather, such an exercise is an obligation of those church authorities who are responsible for choosing new leaders.

Point Two: The parties won't tell everything.

I am not suggesting that the organization or the candidate deliberately mislead each other, though that does happen at times. However, either party might possibly have something that is a weakness and not want to mention it in the search setting. Power politics in the organization, a candidate with a problem spouse—the "hidden" things on both sides can be numerous. Reading resumes and an initial interview typically do not let candidate and committee get familiar enough to relax and become mutually vulnerable. Yet that very vulnerability is the beginning of the trusting relationship essential for success.

Point Three: Time, skill and courage are needed.

Concerning the *time* required, checking references on a candidate may mean contacting four to six people to act as references. Finding those persons available for your phone call may require several other calls, so a total of a dozen calls may be necessary, and each contact could take up to a half hour.

The *skill* needed is in the delicate art of questioning (to be discussed in detail later), but obviously discretion and diplomacy are essential.

The *courage* requirement involves being able to ask probing questions about someone else's life. This is a rare and special kind of courage; not everyone can handle this assignment with the grace that is needed.

Point Four: "Messages from the Lord" are not always confirmed.

When a fellow Christian claims a leading from God about something in his life, we tend to respect that assertion as adequate for his guidance. However, when someone claims divine guidance for the whole search committee, you need to seek additional confirmation to be sure of the source of the message.

I suspect strong personalities are more often involved in these claims than are authentic messages from on high. I say this because, time after time, I have seen key leadership decisions go bad when committee members caved in to a single member's "leading from the Lord." I genuinely believe that, if God chooses to intervene in the search committee's activities, He also knows that a vote will be taken and will be gracious enough to give the message to a majority of the members.

Hard work and logical decisions undergirded by prayer seem to me to be the way God lets us struggle with our leadership decisions in this day and age. For those persuaded otherwise, I can only urge you to take steps ensuring through confirmation that the source of the message is as claimed.

Look for the Flaws
During the face-to-face interview with a candidate, discerning strengths—because they are more or less visible—is easier than perceiving weaknesses or flaws—because they are more or less invisible. Even if or when you spot a flaw, a group interview is an awkward setting in which to ascertain if the perceived weakness does exist and to what degree.

For example, if a college presidency candidate seems to regard fund-raising negatively, or if a pastoral candidate gives visitation duties short shrift, these areas need to be discussed with the references. And if these areas of disinterest or inability are genuine, they should be noted and factored into the overall pattern of strengths and weaknesses.

"Perfect" candidates seldom exist, so you want to identify the weaknesses in advance. Then you can plan to compensate for them. Also, if you know of the limitation before the actual hiring, you will not experience the inevitable disappointment that results when it is discovered later.

Admittedly, *no* candidate is all a search committee wants, but that's a fair state of affairs, because neither is any organization ever all the candidate expects either. Trade-offs in the candidate's strengths and weaknesses to meet the needs of the organization or church are essential, and good reference checking gives a search committee the ability to do this.

Here is a useful rule of thumb concerning flaws: *If you haven't found some flaws, keep on looking!*

How to Handle Sensitive References

A friend who is a sophisticated businessman served on the pastoral selection committee of his church. They carefully checked the references of their leading candidate with sources in the church he was leaving and received very positive answers to their questions. He was called as pastor and they were later dismayed at finding a very different person than had been described to them. After he was terminated they questioned the references they had contacted as to why they had not been more forthright. "We didn't want to keep him from finding another job," came the distressing response.

I do not know if, in this incident, the questions were poorly posed or the respondents lied. Whichever way it happened, the intent to deceive worked, much to the distress of the second congregation. The ethics of the situation obviously forbids lying when a question is asked—though it can and does happen. Yet no one has the responsibility to do more than respond to the question. If a candidate has problems with balky children, a significant health problem or casts a roving eye, telling you those things is not the reference giver's responsibility to tell you unless you ask. Knowing that fact in advance clearly requires that you have a list of questions to pose when you call.

Let's suppose you ask a reference how well the candidate handles his staff and relates to them, and the respondent's written response is "Fairly well." That can be a difficult term to interpret as it lies there on the page, but on the telephone the tone of voice says a lot more. Varying with the inflection, it can mean that a factor is a weakness or that it is a minor strength.

So, *do your reference checking in person or by telephone!*

Professionals in executive search consulting almost never use written references because of their negligible value. Often such references are requested by and then given to the individual involved, which assures that they are not confidential and nothing negative can even be mentioned. A carefully crafted written reference may emphasize a few good things but choose to leave out significant negatives.

Remember, there is no eleventh commandment to tell everything, only the one that says we're not to lie. The Republican political party has it's own eleventh commandment, "Never speak ill of fellow Republicans," and we Christians tend in that direction too, because of our training and culture.

When a reference is given verbally, you can hear the hesitancies, the enthusiasm or lack of it or detect a guardedness. That should prompt you to follow up with other questions in that same interest area. If your follow-on questions finally causes the reference to decline further answers, you can be sure you are into an area that needs more examination with other sources. Keep on checking until you are satisfied that you have as good a grasp as your evaluation requires.

If a source is overseas, and written references are all you have to work with, I suggest you shape the questions and send them with a copy of the position description to the person from whom you are asking the information. When you get the reply, see if you can detect an openness in the responses or if you—in reading between the lines—recognize that they are carefully worded and contain significant omissions.

The task of getting accurate answers to well-thought-out questions may sound to you as if it can become a battle of wits. Indeed, it often is. Tension develops when the source has negative information that he or she does not wish to share, yet you need to have it. Happy, affirming data flows easily but, if you get into the touchy areas, that easy flow slows as resistance develops. Your tactics at this point require some mental toughness as you do several things to obtain what you need.

First, open the reference check with the assurance of absolute confidentiality within the search committee. You may choose to say that the reference will be shared "without attribution." That is, that the reference's name will not be disclosed, even to the search committee, but only identified as "a board member," "a deacon," "a faculty member" or whatever. This assurance can help to loosen up a reluctant source.

And be sure you honor your word when you promise confidentiality!

Second, you can remind the source you are contacting that he is only one of a number of people you are checking with. In effect, you are saying that nothing he or she says will by itself cause the candidate to be dropped. You ease the contact's sense of guilt in this manner.

Third, you can still activate a sense of prospective guilt in references by posing your questions in such a way that they would need to lie, if they did not respond honestly to your questions. While they may not want to damage the candidate's standing they normally will choose to do that rather than lie to you. Awareness of this approach can be a useful insight.

Fourth, if significant negative information develops, get off that particular point as soon as you can and avoid judgmental reactions. Also, be sure to conclude the reference check on an upbeat note.

How to Ask the Questions

As you pose the questions, remember that the first word you use shapes the response. Certain words yield only a yes or no answer. Here are a few examples:

> *Were* you—?
> *Did* he—?
> *Can* he—?
> *Should* he—?
> *If* he—?

Other question starters naturally yield a narrative response that can yield more information, such as:

> *Why* did he—?

How would—?
When—?

If you have an overly chatty source on your hands, use the first group of opening words to control the quantity. The second group can help open up a recalcitrant informant.

Be sure to ask for comparisons from your source. For example:

"How would you rate Dr. Johnson among the various college presidents you have worked with?"

"Would you please identify for me Pastor Gould's most significant strengths and weaknesses?"

Be careful to get an amplification on the answer you get on that question about Pastor Gould's strengths and weaknesses. For instance, are his strengths strong enough to make him successful? Similarly, are his weaknesses possibly so minor that they are negligible and can be ignored?

I frequently use this question with a candidate's former boss:

"If you had the opportunity to whisper in the ear of (the candidate's) new boss, what counsel would you offer that would best bring out this potential and control his limitations?"

Of course, your pencil should be flying as the answers are given, whether in person or over the phone. Do *not* trust your memory.

Remember, recording a phone conversation may be illegal, unless the other party is aware of it. But I believe the request to record diminishes the openness of the responses given. And the use of a speaker phone, so a group can hear the responses, also has a very inhibitory effect on the respondent.

Asking the Unthinkable Questions

As Christians, we know that all sin is abhorrent to God and in His eyes that sins are not large or small, but all are in need of forgiveness. Despite that theological precept, we act on a day-to-day basis as if there were small ones that we should overlook, but big ones we must wrestle with as we unmask them in a candidate's life.

If you found out through references or from the candidate that he formerly had a drinking problem or had been addicted to prescription drugs several years ago, would you consider him further? What if he had been divorced? The list varies from group to group as to what matters would prohibit continued consideration of a candidate. You must decide that for your group.

From the time of King David to this week, some man of God in a leadership role is falling from that role because of a sin revealed to the followers. Human nature being what it is, I know of no way to reliably foretell whom this debacle may hit. However, as a search committee, your duty is to see if there is evidence of any misdeeds in the past that might carry an onus over to your organization.

I am familiar with Christian leaders who have been asked to leave several successive organizations or churches because no reference checks with their prior institutions raised questions in the area of the besetting sin. As Christians, we are not unfamiliar with the sin problem, and we should never assume that our leaders are immune to it. The evidence clearly points to temptations being greater for leaders. That should suggest that a search committee be tough—minded enough to do what it can to ask questions concerning ethics, personal life and other related concerns.

Shortly after a prominent Christian leader was removed from his role, I experimented with a new question to a candidate. I hoped it might avoid a leadership catastrophe, such as had just happened, if this candidate had a real problem. During our interview I said I was beginning with him to bring up a new issue to all candidates for Christian leadership positions. I said to him:

> Friend, if you have anything in your background that has the potential to blow up you and this ministry if it were revealed, I'm sure you don't want to discuss it with me. If by chance this is your situation, I implore you to use any

reason you find convenient to withdraw from further consideration.

The next morning I went to the hotel to take him to a meeting with the search committee. Instead, I found only a note of
explanation left for me, saying that he needed to discipline a part
of his life before he could take on a significant leadership role. I
am still thankful to that man.

---

*Busy Christian leaders have a tough enough
job without the distractions of an inept search
committee tromping into their world. [And]
any leader will tell you that he finds being
sought after a nice compliment, but such an
emotional high is more than offset by the
letdown of a subsequent rejection.*

References to Beware Of

Those of us who make a living that involves reference checking
come to recognize certain types of references that should be
tested before being used:

> *The Hater:* They can't find a good thing to say about the
> candidate. Everything is negative and you wonder what
> motivates this person. As you check with other refer-
> ences, see if you can find out what was wrong between the
> candidate and "the hater." Of course, if all the references
> hate the candidate, don't bother. Just drop the candidate.

> *The Faint Praiser:* You know the phrase, "Damn with faint
> praise." Such praise isn't really support at all but token
> approval and perhaps this reference should be ignored.
> Once again, though, if all the references offer only faint
> praise, dump your candidate.

> *The Cheerleader:* This person thinks the candidate did

everything superbly and seems unable to offer helpful insights beyond effusive support. It makes you wonder if the source is the candidate's best friend, mentor, relative or owes him money.

Keep on checking until you find better references.

What References Should You Seek?

Be sure that a candidate will not knowingly give you the name of a reference that will zing him. Most leaders who have made any difference at all have created enemies or adversaries, whatever the label that is given to their detractors. As I look for outstanding people, I expect to find some detractors and would wonder if some were not present. Try to encourage your candidate to accept this premise and get him to let you talk to a couple of them, as well as his boosters whose names he first provided.

The candidate's relationship with those in authority is an essential reference, so you certainly will want to talk with those to whom your candidate was previously accountable. If your candidate was terminated from that position, you will have some tricky ground to cover, and you may have to determine whether contacts need to be made with various political factions in his former place of employment so as to obtain those needed references from the candidate's superiors.

Peer references can be valuable too. If your candidate is a pastor, how is he regarded by other pastors; or if a president, by other presidents?

Subordinate references are essential if your candidate is to manage other people. If you are looking at a prospective college president, an insight into faculty opinions is needed. When your need is for a parachurch executive, you may wish to ask a financial officer who served under your candidate about his financial knowledge and people-handling skills.

If your organization has denominational ties, you will probably want to get the view of denominational officials of your candidate, too. Remember though, your denomination may have an agenda different from yours that colors their view.

Confidentiality Revisited

At numerous places throughout this book, I mention the need for confidentiality to embrace the total search process. Reference checking offers particularly severe hazards to the confidentiality goal. As important as reference checking is, I urge you to place an even higher value on doing the checking in a manner that avoids disruption of any present ministry your candidate may have. Unless your candidate is unemployed or has an agreement with his board to leave, you face a compelling need to avoid doing anything to upset the people he now leads.

Also, I suggest that your search committee not even contact a prospective candidate until you have done a fair amount of preparatory background checking and referencing. It is callous and un-Christian to generate a candidate's high level of interest in your group and then quickly dump him when you learn something about him that you could have picked up earlier.

Busy Christian leaders have a tough enough job without the distractions of an inept search committee tromping into their world. It takes time to reflect, pray, evaluate and get familiar with the organization doing the recruiting. This diversion of time and energy detracts from their focus on present ministry and can be avoided if, by better preliminary work, the search committee sees that such a pairing will not be a good fit. Any leader will tell you that he finds being sought after a nice compliment, but such an emotional high is more than offset by the letdown of a subsequent rejection.

What Has He Written or Said?

Many pastors or leaders of Christian parachurch groups have put into writing, on cassette or videotape, their best thoughts. Why not have a search committee member check to see if the candidate has written or preached "on the record." Many churches tape every message to share with shut-ins or print up the Sunday sermon. Has your candidate ever written for your denominational periodical? For his seminary, college or Bible school publication? For Christian publications such as *Christianity Today*, *Eternity*, *Moody Monthly* or others? A quick check may reveal he even authored a book.

If you get lucky in this line of inquiry, you can learn quite a bit about your candidate's theology, preaching style and special interests before you ever initiate a contact. And you can save travel, time and the possible embarrassment of turning him down later on.

The Physical Check-up

If a candidate has a medical history or physical condition that may limit his performance or shorten his life expectancy, the hiring organization needs to be aware of that consideration. I know of instances where diabetes, a history of migraine headaches and even cancer has been known in advance, been disregarded—and a successful relationship ensued. I am equally confident that examples of the reverse exist too. However, as long as the condition is revealed before the hiring, the fairness test has been met.

How can you determine the physical fitness of a candidate? The easiest way is to get permission of the candidate to talk with his family physician. The doctor may want written permission to share his patient's medical history with your committee. Be sure also to learn as much as you can—with the candidate's permission—about the health of all his dependents. Serious medical problems anywhere in the family will be likely to have financial and/or psychological effect on the person you are hiring.

A common practice is to require a preemployment physical examination as part of the hiring procedure. You may decide this means is better than talking to the candidate's own doctor, especially if the record reveals no recent physical examinations or treatment.

I remind you that this is an area which may have legal restrictions, and you need to be aware of them. Be careful that you are cognizant of all applicable restrictions by consulting a competent authority.

Psychological Evaluation

In my experience, it is a rarity to request a candidate to undergo a psychological assessment. Unless there is a history of emotional instability in the candidate's past, I see no reason for this procedure.

Credit Check

Not all godly people manage their finances well. Some may even not honor their obligations in a satisfactory manner. If your candidate is precariously in debt or viewed as a poor credit risk, you should know about it in advance. If you decide to hire such a person, doing so will require some planning and precautions.

Commercial credit sources are easily available at minimal cost and I encourage the use of this simple verification. Asking for a credit check is not an unreasonable request of a candidate. Only in rare circumstances will a candidate object to such a request, and if one did object, I would suspect a problem.

You have another available step that can be considered if you feel it necessary. Investigative firms offer services that include both credit checks and finding a record of driving violations or even criminal records. While this action will usually seem an unwarranted step, it may be appropriate in some instances.

Now that you and your committee have completed your research, reference checks, evaluations and investigations, if you are not yet prostrate with exhaustion, you are now ready to consider your new leader's compensation package. Let's take a look at that important item next.

CHAPTER ELEVEN

WHAT IS A GOOD LEADER WORTH?

AFTER 1695 the compensation of [Anglican] clergymen [in Virginia] was fixed by law at 16,000 pounds of tobacco.[1]

Things have changed a great deal since those precolonial days as democracy became the form of government for the emerging nation. Also, representative government moved into most churches and into the processes of self-government, including compensating the clergy.

Discussion about how much to pay those "in the Lord's service" is likely to result in confusion and disagreement. Most Christians are not comfortable discussing this subject. I suspect that this discomfort comes from the unspoken opposing viewpoints often held by the board and the candidate. While many other differences of opinion can be resolved through discussion of the issues, controversy over compensation usually remains unresolved because no one will bring out his real feelings.

Shaping the Compensation Package

Those who do the hiring often have attitudes that result in an inadequate compensation offer to those in Christian service, though this consequence may not be the employers' actual intent. Dr. R.C. Sproul wrote of two such attitudes in his article, "Pastors and Paychecks: Ticket for Low Morale." Stating that employers can display a we-want-to-keep-you-humble attitude, Sproul wisely responds with "we need to understand that it is not our job to enforce other people's voluntary service."[2]

The other attitude he mentions as being widely held is "We don't want to set salaries so high they will attract ministers who are in the ministry for the wrong reason."[3] That's not likely to happen! Almost anyone who can get through a seminary is very likely to do much better financially in any other field. A possible exception is a Ph.D. teaching in a Christian college, tolerating, as such committed academics do, an even worse cost/benefit ratio between education time/expense and career income.

In some circles, I'm sure, the feeling still is that those in ministry will be more deeply spiritual if they can't be sure how their financial needs are going to be met. This thinking is not as pervasive as it once was—at least in my church circles—for which I am thankful as, no doubt, are many ministers.

> I shall never forget how, as a child in a minister's family, I resented our being the recipients of the charity of others and not having things most kids seemed to have. But I will admit it was exciting to "live by faith" and to have to "pray in" food and clothing. In fairness, I must report that I cannot recall ever going to bed hungry—unless it was for disciplinary reasons.

Those in ministry may rightfully have understandable resentments of these attitudes mentioned earlier. The arrogance inherent in them is irritating, to say the least. But people in ministry today are still thought of in two unfortunate categories: (1) They are denied compensation equal to that of others with comparable training, and (2) we expect them to adhere to a higher standard of behavior and conduct than we apply to ourselves.

Another problem for those in ministry is that they are thought of as behaving in bad form even to discuss their com-

"Whatever we decide about the pastor's salary,
let's keep in mind all those sermons last year on
the simple life-style."

Source: *Leadership,* (Summer 1982), p. 69. Reprinted by permission of Larry H. Thomas.

pensation, much less to ask for a raise. Doing so raises the suspicion in others that this person is "materialistic" and "unspiritual."

> I recall how our church in New Jersey was extending a call to a pastor from Michigan to come and lead us. The candidate asked if it would be possible to have an allowance for curtains and drapes because what they had would not fit the new parsonage. That did it for one church member with a very strong personality. He convinced a majority of the congregation that this request was a sign of an unspiritual man. The offer was retracted and this action had a very negative effect on the candidate's present church, which had learned of the offer and of his intention to leave.

Most people in ministry are not only reluctant to bring up their financial needs, but they are also unskilled in negotiating such matters. The search committee, on the other hand, possibly has among its members either a lawyer, a personnel officer or a businessman, all of whom are skilled negotiators. The contest is unfair and can cause the candidate to feel defensive and uncertain.

A sensitive search committee will sense such feelings and dissipate them by being supportive and open in the discussions. The mutual intent should be to cover aspects of compensation during the discussions. Certainly, not all points will meet the candidate's desires, but they should be covered so that no later charge can be made that they had been overlooked.

Perhaps the term "negotiations" sounds strange in Christian circles, but it shouldn't. Negotiation does not imply an adversarial relationship, but rather that there can be give-and-take in the discussions as they lead to agreement. A church search committee should have no feeling of desiring to "drive a hard bargain" with the candidate. If either party concludes negotiations with a "winner" feeling, the other may well feel it is the "loser" and carry hard feelings into the relationship that is just beginning. Considerable thought should precede the compensation negotiations to assure that all issues are covered and that the result is a win-win result.

Vows of Poverty or $1,600,000 a Year?

Some Catholic orders for centuries have required vows of poverty. I am amazed and inspired to see able people take such vows because of their love of Christ. I can almost hear some others, also in active ministry, saying, "I didn't take a vow of poverty, but it's turned out that way anyway."

I am even more amazed that Jim and Tammy Bakker can preach about a Savior who had no earthly possessions while, at the same time, taking $1,600,000 out of their PTL ministry during 1986! Obviously, the earnings of everyone else in ministry must fall somewhere between that of the Bakkers and those who take poverty vows.

The ostentatious life-styles of some Christian leaders— thankfully, a very few—have not raised the ire of their followers as much as I would have suspected. To me, this shows how little thought has been given to a theology of compensation and stewardship. Prominent lay leaders and clergy sit on the boards of these flagrantly overpaying ministries, yet they seem to lack the courage to challenge those actions. Such an abdication of their spiritual and fiduciary responsibilities should cause universal outrage, a donor revolt and a close scrutiny by regulatory authorities. The growing watchdog role of the Evangelical Council for Financial Accountability should help curb this form of financial abuse, as well as others.

Raising/Begging Your Own Support

It is quite common in Christian ministry to serve with a "faith" ministry. That's shorthand for "We have no money to pay you, so go out and raise your own support and then you can minister with us." Many mission boards and parachurch organizations have operated successfully for many years in this fashion, among them, Campus Crusade, Wycliffe Bible Translators, Mission Aviation Fellowship, InterVarsity Christian Fellowship, Africa Inland Mission, Youth for Christ and others.

The linguist, pilot, evangelist, doctor or youth worker

spends from six months to as long as it takes to put together a financial support package of the required amount. These candidates may get a little training and coaching from their sponsoring organization in how to do this fund-raising—"deputation work"—and off the young couple goes, while grandparents or friends watch the kiddos. Hopefully, they put together the needed support with the help of a number of churches and personal friends, with their home church providing the largest amount. Very few candidates have personal resources to provide their own support after years of college, Bible school or seminary, flight training and the like.

Some high-quality candidates for Christian service shy away from such faith ministries because of this self-financing requirement. Either they cannot accept the financial uncertainty of it or they see the support-formation period as personally demeaning, a form of Christian begging. The successful candidates see it as an opportunity for the donor to vicariously share in their ministry through financial stewardship, even if the donors themselves cannot go.

In recent years such faith ministries have had to add to the fund-raising burdens of their staff people by including the cost of retirement, travel and furlough and even a share of the operational and overhead expense of the ministry. In 1988, the Ministry Partnership Plan of Mission Aviation Fellowship called for each new couple to target a goal of $4,000 per month in donor support. While that seems a staggering sum at first glance, it is only half the cost per staff person when aircraft purchase and operational costs are included.

I salute those who serve in such faith ministries. Their commitment is such that their faith is apparent in their pocketbooks as they risk it all for the sake of Christ.

Tentmakers

This term "tentmakers" covers those who minister while supporting themselves, as Paul did when he interspersed his missionary activities with times when he reverted to his trade to finance his next trip. (see Acts 18:1-3).

A carpenter or teacher who works in those callings while

being a part-time pastor without a salary is a tentmaker. So is the engineer who goes abroad as employee of an international company and uses all his spare time to minister in that country.

A form of tentmaker is the wife who works to help support the family while her husband is in ministry at a less-than-adequate salary. She may well be continuing a pattern of ministry support that began when they were newlyweds in Bible school or seminary.

Paying the Pastor or President

If your church, college or parachurch organization is planning to recruit a new leader but lacks the financial resources to pay

"Only the true Church, the body of believers, is assured continuity by God. I cannot believe that God is pleased with the plethora of competing and overlapping ministries that compete for funds as they confuse and weary prospective donors and those considering a life of Christian ministry."

that person a living wage, you have a real challenge on your hands. You need a person of uncommon talent and courage who feels strongly led of God to your post, despite the financial problems. Before you couch your leadership need in spiritual terms to challenge a likely candidate, ask yourself some tough questions.

Peter Drucker, the prominent management consultant, has said, "Religious organizations have remarkable renewal abilities. But this does not [necessarily] mean they are divinely ordained."[4] For what good reasons should your church or ministry be kept alive, if financial support is so lacking? Are you no longer meeting a real need?

Organizations tend to live beyond their usefulness and only the true Church, the body of believers, is assured continuity by God. Denominations, colleges, churches and independent ministries will come and go, and that fact should not surprise us. I

cannot believe that God is pleased with the plethora of competing and overlapping ministries that compete for funds as they
confuse and weary prospective donors and those considering a
life of Christian ministry.

The salary: How much?

While salary is the largest part of the compensation package, it
is only one of a number of elements. But let's deal with it first.

If your church is new, still small and has only a small salary to
offer, you may have to settle for a part-time person. Either your
pastor will serve two churches, have a secular part-time job, will
serve you while getting his theological training, or also will teach
in a Bible school, college or seminary.

If your church has grown to a congregation of 80-100 members, you ought to be able to afford a pastor of your own, and, as
the membership grows, so will the requirements of the job and
the compensation. Here are questions to ask as you seek the
answer on how much to pay:

- What can the church afford?
- What experience are your requiring?
- What salaries are other churches of your denomination and
  size paying?
- What special conditions do you have that must be consid-
  ered, such as elevated housing costs, no available jobs for
  the spouse, etc.?
- What was the departing pastor paid?
- What are the other church staff paid, if you have any?

Size and location of the ministry obviously make a big difference. The Presbyterian church in rural Templeton, California is
quite small, despite its long history, and the pastor's modest salary is subsidized by the concerned and supportive Presbytery of
Santa Barbara. In the midst of affluent, crowded Orange County,
in southern California, is St. Andrews in Newport Beach, a
large, thriving evangelical Presbyterian church with a staff of 32,
of which seven are pastors. While the job descriptions of the

leader of each church may sound generally the same, the specific requirements are quite different, as is the salary.

As you look at what you paid your last pastor, scrutinize it carefully. Did you give him salary increases regularly, so that you kept up with prevailing salaries? If not, you have some catching up to do and perhaps a note of apology should be sent to your former pastor.

Also, if you are going to look for all the experience and skills of your former leader, you should expect to pay 10 percent to 20 percent more to your new minister, because you want to provide a financial incentive to make the move. While ministry reasons may be the major reason for such a move, a salary increase is appropriate.

Some denominations place requirements on their churches that they meet at least the established minimum salary level plus mandated plans, such as retirement plan contributions.

"The traditions of the American Church seem to include getting all the free labor possible from the pastor's wife. [But] women's liberation and recent legislation have persuaded even chauvinistic churches to view the wife in a different light."

While we are on the subject, if your annual salary increases are less than the annual cost-of-living figure, you are decreasing your leader's income. If you want to keep him, give an increase of at least that much with deserved merit increases on top of that. If you don't plan to give cost-of-living increases, perhaps a change is in order.

For some of your overseas missionaries, the soft U.S. dollar is financially killing them. This was not so until a few years ago, and church missions committees need to be up-to-date on currency problems, if overseas ministries are not to be starved out.

How can you find out what comparable churches are paying their pastors? Go ask them. If you are in a denomination, compensation surveys probably are available with a complete listing of all forms of compensation.

If you are independent, ask other independent churches for their annual report and do a little figuring, if they don't want to tell you. Or, ask a nearby Bible school or seminary what it will take to attract a person such as you seek. They will be better informed about salaries of recent graduates, but they can be helpful nevertheless.

Does her income count?
The traditions of the American Church seem to include getting all the free labor possible from the pastor's wife. As times have changed, a substantial number of ministers' wives now are in the work force. Also, women's liberation and recent legislation have persuaded even chauvinistic churches to view the wife in a different light, one where she is a person in her own right rather than a tag-along bonus. Unless you are hiring a husband-and-wife team as co-pastors, which is happening increasingly now, and which the Salvation Army has always done, you are hiring *only* the husband. If for some reason you do not wish the wife of a candidate to work and she now has an income, you should add that amount into your computation of what they need to live on.

A friend of mine said that a search committee told him that they would prefer that their pastor's wife not have a job of her own. He responded, "That's fine with us if you will set aside a fund for our children's college education, because that's where her earnings go."[5]

When you consider salary, there are several factors that influence what the figure should be. For example, if you are in Wisconsin and are making an offer to a Florida pastor, don't forget that there is a significant difference in the personal income between the two states.

How much should you weigh the individual circumstances of candidates? If you know his wife "comes from money," should you offer less? If they have two kids in college, does the greater need influence your decisions? Or does a handicapped child whose care is expensive? Does a childless couple warrant as high an offer as a family with six kids?

In the business world, the salary is attached to the job, not to the individual's need. Some Christian groups, however, such as Campus Crusade, have allowances that vary with the number of dependent children. So does the military and our welfare system. Your search committee must decide how you view this matter. Good organizational theory is not always an adequate answer to such questions.

Recently I heard about a church in Texas that compensates the pastor as a percentage of the church's income. Even if an upper limit is placed on what could be earned, I view this plan as reprehensible. It encourages irresponsible actions and provides the wrong motivation. I can't help wonder if the board making the offer is dominated by people who sell insurance or Amway products?

Other needed tools
In any professional job there are other forms of compensation to allow the person to do the job well. Blue-collar jobs may provide tools, uniforms and always the materials to work with plus periodic training to acquire new needed skills. Executive positions provide cars, country clubs, health exams, financial counseling and other perks.

Ministers have needs for tools too. They are:

- a car or car allowance (he has to drive to do church business);
- book and periodical allowance (if he stops reading, you will soon be asleep in the pews); and
- paid study leave (help him grow and avoid burnout).

You may think of others.

Fringe benefits
What were once called "fringe benefits" now have the word "fringe" dropped because they are well-established by practice and are now so expensive in the aggregate that they can be 30-50 percent of salaries. The benefits are even more when the salaries are quite low, for example:

- Housing or housing allowance. The manse or parsonage seems to be a vanishing practice that is being replaced by housing allowances. Tax law gives ministers a favored treatment, so don't put all the income into the salary. With a parsonage, a utilities allowance is normal, plus a sum for maintaining it.
- Health insurance for the whole family, fully paid (a very expensive item).
- Vacation, usually three to four weeks a year, plus an agreed number of times that he can be absent to speak elsewhere, attend denominational meetings and the like.

  Preachers usually get at least a month of vacation while teachers get three months. Why is it that we give more vacation to the people who can't afford to take them?
- Retirement plan. Most denominations have a mandatory pension program and require the church to pay from half to all of the cost. It's better for the church to pay it with pretax dollars than the pastor with his taxed income.

  Responsible church leadership has increasingly recognized how important it is to have adequate financial support for retired pastors and their wives. The cause of Christ has been embarrassed too often by elderly clergy who were destitute.

  My own father was a preacher who had no interest in planning for his financial future because "the Lord will provide." When he died at age 69, he still had never owned a house, nor had a place to which he could retire. The remembrance of that makes me sad and a little angry, even now, many years later.

The relocation

The matter of relocation gets tricky. Did you know that when you pay for the relocation expense of your new leader, he will pay a tax on that amount? To avoid that unintended tax liability, you may wish to offset it with an amount equal to the tax.

As you relocate your new spiritual shepherd to your area, you may be amazed by the costs that must be faced. The idea is to make the new pastor whole for the costs of moving to your area. Here are some items to be discussed:

- The cost of the moving firm's service. Will you include the packing service, insurance during transit, the extra fee to insure on-schedule delivery?
- The sales commission for selling the house they are leaving.
- Closing costs on the new house.
- Telephone and utilities installation connection charges (since deregulation telephone costs are distressingly high).
- Car registration fees and drivers' licenses, if they come from a different state.
- Any increased insurance cost on the car(s), if you moved them to an area with a higher rate.
- Real estate tax increases, if any.
- An allowance for the new drapes/curtains (the old ones never fit a new house).
- Costs of moving pets, a second car and other items.

Concerning the actual moving costs, you want to make a "lump sum" offer. That is, get several movers' bids and pay the average as a lump sum, thus leaving your new family with the option of using the money in the best way possible. For example, maybe the old washer could be left behind and the moving money used toward buying a new one. Perhaps the now infrequently used weight-lifting equipment may also be wise to leave behind. The money made available allows a beneficial purging of junk for a fresh start. The business world uses this plan a lot.

The trickiest part of handling relocation costs may be in the area of real estate. Candidates from Spokane, Dayton, Chattanooga or Buffalo will go into shock when they see housing costs in Pasadena, Wilmette, Stamford, Lexington, Palo Alto or McLean. If you desire a candidate from a low-cost real estate area and you are in a high-cost area, tighten your belt and dig down deeply. You will need to provide real estate help in any of a variety of ways, unless you provide a manse. Loans, grants, a housing allowance increase or buying them a house are only part of the possibilities. Good luck.

Leaving the parsonage

From time to time, a candidate you are considering will presently be living in housing provided by the church or college. But your church does not have a house to provide, so a problem has to be faced. Your committee may now lack the resources to provide a house or you may feel it unwise to do so, in any case.

So, what do you do? I wish I had some sage counsel for you, but I do not. I can only recommend that you seek financial and real estate counsel as you seek a solution. A wise search committee could even assess the church's available resources and position on this matter as the search begins, not after you are already attracted strongly to an outstanding candidate. This foresight can save you a lot of unnecessary wear and tear later.

Miscellaneous Thoughts on Compensation

Termination provisions. A thoughtful search committee may wish to include in the offer letter some arrangements in case the pastor is terminated, but not if he quits. Unhappy congregations have a tendency to be less than generous with a pastor they are terminating and can get really nasty when they feel betrayed. We all know this, but no one thinks of this when the romance of the hiring process is going on. Would it be productive for a progressive separation payment to be arranged? It could range from two months after only a year to a year after 10 years of service.

Uninterrupted medical insurance. If your new pastor and his family were at his prior church for five years, it's possible that some new medical problem developed during that time. If so, it is important to keep their medical/hospitalization coverage with the same carrier. A new application could result in a "preexisting condition" exclusion that could cause financial havoc.

Salary reviews. You should plan to include in your offer letter a statement that his salary will be reviewed annually. That does not assure he will get an increase, just that he will be carefully reviewed. If you have an evaluation system or performance appraisal procedure operating at your church or college, you may want to relate the annual salary review to the performance appraisal.

Outside income. Your pastor will usually be given an honorarium to perform weddings, funerals and such. Also, when he preaches elsewhere he will be paid for it. Be sure you have a clear understanding that these are his to keep. Also, if he authors a book or articles, the income should be his to keep—unless he did the writing on church time.

An Attitude Toward Money

I'm not a psychologist, but I suspect that the experiences of our formative years shape our underlying values toward money and the things it allows us to do. If we are an anxious, worry-prone type of personality, that also colors our view of money and the related need for security. These attitudes are carried over in the adult years of ministry and are either altered or reinforced by the person we marry.

A search committee should be interested in a candidate's attitude toward money; that is, financial security, desires for material things and other facets of life that relate to having or not having money. As you look for the value systems of the candidate and wife, inquire into their family background and their socio-economic roots so that you can discover where they are now. Some people will have come from an affluent background and still yearn for it, while others from it have opted for a more simple life-style. A candidate from a poor family may be attracted to wealth and show a desire to associate with those who possess it, though not necessarily so.

If you can understand this aspect of your candidates you will be learning about their basic values and their ego needs. This knowledge equips you to better determine how well the candidate will relate to your college, church or parachurch organization.

In Jay Kesler's book, *Being Holy, Being Human,* he deals with this subject. He points out that ministers are often given favors or gifts by affluent parishioners that can cause those church members "to begin to think, often in subtle and even unconscious ways, that to a certain extent they own you. There can even develop a bit of condescending attitude. Pastors can begin to feel like beggars, beholden to the generosity of these people."[6]

Jay points out that the frustration of feeling financially second-class can cause a combative defensiveness toward the more affluent members. Such ministers can feel, "In preaching about total dedication and giving your all to the Lord, it's not hard to tell when they're really making a veiled statement to the effect that some people in the congregation are making a lot of money, but they can't be as spiritual as I am or they wouldn't have so much."[7]

It is neither a sin nor a virtue for a candidate to be thrifty or even cheap. Nor is it necessarily bad to be a little extravagant, spending almost all you earn. However, you need to know if your candidate is either of those in advance so you can be sure he will be well-accepted.

> In a secular search assignment I found a candidate who was excellent, but references said he had the annoying habit of nickel and diming his employer on his expense accounts. I found this habit came from a family background with a father who was in a WWII concentration camp where he almost starved to death. My candidate's job was saved when he showed this same practice with my client who now expected it, understood it and told him to knock it off.

Jay Kesler speaks of a minister who said his biggest challenge was to "get a raise without making people angry."[8] If you understand your candidate's view of money, you will be prepared for his later actions and able to take corrective action if it is needed.

If a new leader has a contentious attitude toward his compensation, it could be that he feels he negotiated poorly and now resents that fact and the financial pressure it puts on his family.

The Offer Letter

While verbal agreements have legal standing, they usually lead to misunderstandings. So *put everything in writing* before you expect a firm answer from your candidate. The letter may be from the chair of the search committee, but it should also be signed by the chair of the board. This shows that the terms and conditions the letter lays out are authorized by the board as well as the search committee. After all, the search committee is quickly dismissed as the search concludes and the board is the continuing ruling body.

Offer letters should include a starting date, details of compensation and a clear statement about the duration of the offer. The year-to-year contract is a demeaning device that serves to keep the leader insecure. Hopefully, you do not have such an old-fashioned arrangement. Colleges and parachurch organizations will often use three-year or five-year contracts while churches usually have an open-ended arrangement that continues until either party terminates it.

Some stipulation is appropriate concerning the notice required when the relationship is to be terminated. Also, it could avoid a possible misunderstanding, if you clarify whether you allow the accruing of unused sick leave, vacation or study leave from year to year. Try to provide solutions in advance to questions that may raise controversy when your leader leaves. It is simple then to refer to the prorating of compensation and benefits in case of a termination in the offer letter.

To summarize:

"The laborer is worthy of his hire," Scripture tells us in Luke 10:7. While that is surely true, the verse can be interpreted so variously that it provides me with no helpful light for this chapter. My plea is that greater attention be paid to this neglected aspect of compensating Christian leadership. The Christian faith emphasizes care and concern of fellow believers and treating employees fairly. This ethic should set the stage for an openness in discussing compensation that will remove the queasiness which often characterize board—candidate discussions.

Few areas of Christian activities have retained out-of-date attitudes as much as the compensating of those in ministry. A rethinking is overdue. Let that rethinking begin with you and your church or organization.

Notes

1. Daniel J. Boorstin, *The Americans,* vol. 1, *The Colonial Experience* (New York: Random House, Inc., 1958).
2. R.C. Sproul, "Pastors and Paychecks," *Eternity,* May 1988. Used by permission.
3. Ibid.
4. Peter Drucker, "Drucker on Religious Organizations" in "Musings of the Sage," *Reflections from the Lamp* 3 (Winter 1987): 2.
5. Quoted in "The Minister's Own Marriage," *Theology, News and Notes,* June 1988. Used by permission of Dr. Duane Alleman, Pacific Psychological Resources, Pasadena, CA.
6. Jay Kesler, *Being Holy, Being Human* (Carol Stream, IL: Christianity Today, Inc., 1988). Used by permission.
7. Ibid.
8. Jay Kesler, *Being Holy.* Used by permission.

CHAPTER TWELVE

WRAPPING UP THE SEARCH AND WELCOMING THE NEW LEADER

HE accepted," cried the exultant search committee chairman to his committee members.

The members' responses ranged from "praise the Lord," to "what a relief," all uttered with deep feeling. Then, as the happy conversation ebbed, someone asked, "What do we do now?"

The chairman, a battle-scarred veteran of two prior searches, said, "As happy an event as this is, our work is not done yet. There are still four tasks." He then outlined their task of communicating their selection to the organization, signing off those who were not selected, preparing for the actual arrival of the new leader and his family, saying "thanks" to a lot of people and writing a history of the search.

Remember when you got engaged? If you are at all like me, you wanted to tell everyone the good news, even some who didn't really care. Although in quite a different situation, a search committee member is tempted to act like the newly-engaged fellow. The search is over and the long-sought person not only has been found, but has accepted the proposal to spend the future years together! Also, the committee member can now spend more time with the family and can at long last share with the spouse all that has been going on for this many months.

If only it was all that simple!

First, when is the person just selected agreeable for the announcement to be made? He may still need to inform his board and staff of this development, and your premature announcement could damage his departure or even that ministry. Those discussions he has yet to hold can have major unanticipated effects. For example, if the discussions go poorly and acrimony develops, he may be told to leave now. You should be ready for that. Or, they may plead that he stay until they find his replacement because they would "fall apart" without a strong leader. That could cause a three- to six-month delay, an event you should try to forestall, yet be ready for it if it happens.

Second, your search committee members will find it tougher to maintain the needed confidentiality during this acceptance-to-announcement period than at any other time, I suspect. Don't permit them to lower their guard.

Third, the worst possibility is that your new leader succumbs to the entreaties of his present organization and recants his decision. This happens fairly regularly in the business world as the candidate accepts a promotion and raise to stay on and smilingly says, "Sorry" to the prospective employer.

> This "worst possibility" happened in a pastoral search where I chaired the committee. When I got the recanting telephone call, after he had a 98 percent affirming vote from the congregation and it had all been announced, I was furious! I flew across the country to confront him and get a reversal of his reversal. I failed, but it proved to be a blessing. A year or so later, he was forced to leave the church that he "couldn't leave" and we learned that he would not have fitted our needs.

"I like to think of myself as the facilitator and enabler of this church rather than the senior pastor or chief executive officer."

Source: *Leadership,* Fall 1984, p. 82. Reprinted by permission of Rob Portlock.

All of this says loudly, *be sure you really have your choice wrapped up before you dismiss the other candidates!*

Signing off the Candidates

By "signing off," I mean contacting all the individuals you have been in touch with about being a candidate for the position you are trying to fill. If you look at the search process as ministry, as it should be regarded, you should be caring as much for "the ninety and nine" candidates you will dismiss as you do for the one you select.

Four principles should guide your committee in its sign-offs:

1. You owe a response to every person you contacted.
If you generated interest on that person's part, he has spent time and energy in thought, prayer, family consultation and preparing a resume or forms and so on. For that he deserves your acknowledgment and thanks. Incredibly, I hear of continuing instances of search committees not extending this basic courtesy. Even those who decline interest initially, I believe, warrant a thank-you note. Also, they may have been helpful sources for the qualified candidate you need.

2. Do it as quickly as possible.
If your committee is sure that a candidate will not fit your need, why wait? If your candidate is actively looking for a new position, he is waiting anxiously to hear from you. To make him wait unnecessarily is an inconvenience at the least and a source of distress at the worst. Sign-offs will be needed over a long period of time, beginning when you first review the collected resumes/dossiers. From then on, other sign-offs will be needed as new contacts are made and candidates are found not to be suitable.

3. Do it honestly.
If a candidate got to the interview stage, I believe that the sign-off letter should be personalized with a review of the things that were seen as strengths and also an explanation of the basis for the negative decision. The review of the positives serves to preserve the person's dignity and to reassure him about his gifts

being favorably perceived. When a candidate is selected, seldom does he ask why it happened. But when a candidate is disqualified, that question always arises. The candidate wants to know if he was somehow at fault and what this could mean to him in future interviews with other committees. If you can, try to help the dismissed candidate have a growth experience out of this encounter.

Leave the candidate as well of as he was when you first met him. To do this successfully requires some planning, an inherent respect for the candidate and a sensitivity to the feelings of others. If possible, your dealings with candidates should not result in a win-lose situation, but in a win-win one with no losers.

If possible, I would encourage you to have a discussion of your criteria and the candidate's apparent shortcomings on a candid basis. Few committee members will have the courage to take this approach, I realize, and some with the needed courage may not have the skills to do it well. However, the possible benefit to the committee may be that the ensuing discussion will clarify some areas of misunderstanding which would move the dismissed candidate back into active consideration. I have had this happen numerous times. Unsuccessful candidates often have a valid lament when they say they were given only superficial polite reasons, not the "real ones."

Evasiveness is often transparent, I find, and it is often more satisfying to bring out real concerns and discuss them, as difficult as that may be.

4. Leave the candidate as well off as he was when you first met him.

To do this successfully requires some planning, an inherent respect for the candidate and a sensitivity to the feelings of others. If possible, your dealings with candidates should not result in a win-lose situation, but in a win-win one with no losers. It takes extra effort and some creativity to pull that off, I realize.

A moment ago I called for honesty in the feedback to dismissed candidates, but that can easily clash with handling candidates with sensitivity. Don't you at times withhold "honest opinions" from loved ones for reasons of kindness? Neither should you be so "honest" with a candidate that you are hurtful.

You should *never* bring up a negative factor if it can't be changed. Could the candidate improve the quality of his voice if you told him you thought it was thin and nasal? Could age, obesity, an unacceptable spouse, a flat personality, a regional accent or many other perceived deficiencies be changed if you told the candidate? Certainly not. If you did mention such a matter, would it be a surprise? I expect not, and that the candidate has tried to do all he could do to correct the problem. If you feel I am now recommending a form of evasiveness, I will plead that it is of value to be sensitive and considerate.

Most gaffes in the sign-off process are unintentional, I am sure, but it takes good planning to avoid them. A committee member with good writing skills should be teamed with one with good verbal skills to handle the task. The sign-off letter used at early stages of the search should be that writer's best effort and reviewed by the chairman. A well-done form letter will do if individually typed and addressed. It should honor the candidates and bring credit to the organization doing the search.

Later on in the search, with the candidates who have been interviewed, individual letters are needed. You may wish to extend an invitation to discuss any questions the ex-candidate may have. They can be referred to the committee member with the good verbal skills.

I share with you an experience of what can happen if care is not taken in handling sign-offs. A friend of mine who has been a successful Christian college president told this humorous story to me, though it was devastating to him at the time.

Bob was one of a number of candidates carefully wooed and interviewed as the prospective president for a well-regarded Christian college. He says, "I wasn't selected, which was fine because they chose an excellent man.

When the selection was made, an announcement was sent out widely, including one to me. It said that the person selected was 'head and shoulders above all the other candidates.' That really hurt."

Bob laughed at the conclusion of the story, but even years later the memory of this insensitive act bothered him.

My prize for inconsiderate handling of candidates goes to one of my favorite Christian colleges, located in the Pacific Northwest. Their search for a new president faltered after the candidates met with representatives of the faculty, the students and the administrative staff, who were all unimpressed.

As the search committee began again, the chairman saw the need to let all the college family and friends know that the search was to start over. His comments were printed in the college newspaper which named their candidates and their current affiliations. The renewed search effort was greatly complicated when the chairman said of the candidates and their campus visit, "What we saw didn't warrant making either one of the candidates president of _____ College. The committee's decision was confirmed by evaluations from students, faculty and staff."

I know the committee chairman is a loving man and a fine pastor, but his unwise disclosure became a public condemnation. The candidates had every right to be furious, and the published comment became an indictment of the college as either cruel or thoughtless. Earlier in the book I stressed the need for confidentiality in the search process, and this incident could have been avoided by not using names, though it still would have been insensitive. As it was handled, the college was fortunate not to have had a contact from the dismissed candidates' attorneys.

"We Selected—"

We have just discussed at length handling sign-offs of the candidates. This next suggestion will sound like too much additional work, but I urge your committee to consider it. The people dismissed at the first review of credentials probably have an under-

standable interest in whom you finally chose. Why not tell them
with a short note, which can be an individually addressed form
letter? Remember all the sources you asked for recommendations of possible candidates? They, too, should get a note of
thanks and learn whom you selected, don't you think?

At the risk of making this burden intolerable, I suggest
another category of people whose help was indispensable and
who should be thanked. They are the people who provided the
references on your candidates. It's logical to thank the references of the person you selected, but I suggest you also thank
those who provided insights into those you did not choose. In a
way, their opinions were just as important as the references on
the person you chose. Hopefully, you will find a way to say you
regarded highly the candidate you discussed with them and that
the selection of someone else was in no way an adverse reflection on them. This kindness by you may restore a little of the
lost lustre of a candidate who wasn't the winner.

Thanking Your Committee Members
As chairman of the search committee, you will want to do something to express your thanks to your committee members,
assuming you are still speaking to each other. More appropriately, the board of the church, college or parachurch organization
should find a way to recognize the arduous labors of the committee. If your search process has gone like most do, you have
shared, prayed and worked together so long and so closely that
you have forged new and lasting friendships.

Never Again?
If you are ever called upon to serve on a search committee a
second time, I hope you will not say, "Never again!" A major
problem with most search committees is that they are always
comprised of amateurs and usually beginners. To minimize this
problem, I strongly recommend that a post-mortem be held by
the selection committee and a written record be prepared of how
the search process worked. Specific notes should be made about
the things that were particularly productive and, similarly, the
things that went wrong.

Normally, your organization will not need to find a new leader again for at least 10 or 15 years. By then most of your current selection committee will probably be unavailable to serve again and, without your valuable written case history, the new committee is doomed to repeat all or most of the errors that yours made.

The Welcoming

Now that the new pastor or president has been selected, who is in charge of the process of getting him and his family "on board"? It varies, depending on the organization and situation. Sometimes the search committee takes the lead, but it could be the responsibility of the ruling board. Often the tasks are divided and delegated to those groups or individuals who have the gift of hospitality. There is enough work to give everyone a piece of it, I assure you.

Continuing communication

The new leader and his family are now caught in two contrasting sets of feelings. Leaving old friends, valued co-laborers, a familiar neighborhood and a personal support group is hard to do. Emotionally, it can be very draining and depressing. The other set of feelings can be ones of excitement, challenge and trepidation, as the new place of service is visualized. The hiring church or college should be sensitive to these opposing tugs, one of the heart and the other more of the mind. Let's hope they can provide more positive, encouraging things to look forward to than there are sad events of withdrawal where your new leader and his family are saying farewell.

Anxiety about the future is natural and it can best be diminished by having someone to talk to who knows the new situation. The new organization should have a contact person who is readily available to answer any question or concern the new pastor or president may have. It is best if this person is not the board chairman or other authority figure. Rather, select a friendly person who enjoys such a helping role and who would be free from the role of being a boss of the new leader. This person should call now and then to chat, to keep the incoming pastor aware of events in the church and to be an available listening ear.

The president's or pastor's new job is full of exciting new challenges that should make his adrenalin flow. He feels good about the affirmation of the call he has accepted and should have a new sense of being in a significant place of service.

But what about his wife and children? For the wife, the transitional tasks are formidable and her goal is to restore the stability and normality of the new home. Depending on their ages and personalities, the move to a new community can be either easy or traumatic.

I suggest that a caring, thoughtful group of people will seek to meet the needs of *all* members of the incoming family. Certainly, if the family members are unhappy, it impacts the effectiveness of the new leader.

A survey of a number of Christian leaders' wives and families revealed some of the problems that can develop. An example: A child of a couple serving with a missionary organization became severely disturbed. Later, as he was in therapy, he said that his folks moved because they thought it was God's will and failed to consider the needs of their children.

When God's special servants are called to move long distances or to different cultures, they can pay a high personal price, and one they may not have foreseen. When you have elderly parents, particularly if they are in poor health, relocating is hard. So, too, is relocating when your kids are in junior high or high school years.

Such families need an unusual amount of support from the new church. And even more in need of support are those who left their children behind: Their nest is now empty for the first time, there are no friends yet in the new setting, and the husband is so busy on his new job that he has little time for his wife and the myriad of coping problems facing her.

A good friend of mine is the wife of the president of a prominent parachurch organization. I assisted in their coming from the other side of the globe to minister in the U.S., and their children stayed behind to finish school or to get on with their lives in their own country. While she now feels acclimated to the U.S.A. and believes they are where God wants them, she misses her family and grandchild tremendously. There is a serious undertone in her comment as she humorously says to me, the recruiter, "Thanks, Bob, for messing up my life."

What can be done to help the family members in such a situation? If you are sensitive enough to seek out such problems, you are probably well-equipped to provide some helpful answers. If possible, provide a person who can become a real friend to the newcomer. Before a real friendship can develop, two or three people may need to make an investment of time and energy. If possible, find out what the wife's best friend was like "back home" and see if you have anyone similar in your fellowship. With teenagers, the same idea is appealing but the social dynamics of that age cause me to doubt it will work.

During the month or two between the time the call was extended and when the leader and his family arrive on the scene, it would be as helpful for the wife—as it was for the husband—to have a phone friend in the new place that she could call with her own questions and concerns.

Moving vans and related traumas

If you have ever moved to a new community, you later shared stories with others who have moved about all the things that went wrong. The late arrival, damaged and lost goods, claims to be made, the demand for cash payment late at night—those and other tests of your patience, sanity and Christian grace.

You can assist your incoming family greatly by trying to anticipate the physical problems of the move.

By all means, have a couple of people available at the house to help out the day the movers come. Life has few days that are more hectic than this one. Arrange for meals and if the beds aren't in place when exhaustion hits everyone, find them other sleeping quarters. Also, be sure the electricity, gas, water and telephone are all working when the van arrives.

Provided housing

Although the practice is declining, many churches and colleges still provide a parsonage, manse or president's residence. If that is your practice, try to have things ready for the new family. See that everything is in working order, do the painting or papering to freshen things up and try to make your new leader's family feel welcome in a practical way.

Naturally, it would be desirable to ask the homemaker about her choices for the colors, fabrics and the like, because it is to be her home.

For the new pastor or president, "installation" means the big formal ritual that starts his ministry. For his wife, "installation" has a more practical meaning of getting the washer and dryer working.

Don't forget to fill the cupboards for them. No one brings bread, milk, sugar and peanut butter with them.

No matter what you do in advance, many things remain undone and help is usually welcomed. Dixie Bolinder is the wife of Reverend Garth Bolinder, pastor of Hillcrest Covenant Church near Kansas City. Like most ministerial families, they have moved a few times. Here is a story of hers.

> Once when we moved, I had a friend call to say she was coming over but not to talk or visit. "What do you need done?" she asked me. I told her I still needed the grout cleaned in the bathroom.
> "Good," she said, "I'll be right over." That was the most wonderful gesture. She just took it in her own hands and helped. I'll never forget it.[1]

House hunting

When it isn't provided, finding suitable housing can be a grueling and disappointing task. If your search committee leveled with the candidate, it was frank with him about real estate costs in your area. But if the committee did not and a shock over the high cost of housing awaits the new family, a pall is immediately cast over the beginnings of the new relationship.

The newcomers quickly need to learn about schools, transportation and other factors that impact a house-buying decision. Present two competent real estate agents and let your new pastor choose whom he wants to use. If the realtors are from the church, protect the pastor from a political hassle as he gets started in his ministry.

Being a "Welcome Wagon"

When you are a stranger in town and have a household to run, knowing how to get started is hard. You need a kind of "Welcome Wagon" to assist you as you settle in.

> In 1987, Bob and Margaret Ann Seiple moved from suburban Philadelphia to southern California, where he assumed the presidency of World Vision (U.S.). She relates, "A neighbor, who was not associated with World Vision, simply took over and told me what I needed to know. She made a map of the places I needed to go to and how long it took to get there. It was very thoughtful."

Lots of questions face the newcomer:

> "Where can we find a good dentist?"
> "Is there a good mechanic where I can take my car?"
> "Who is a good OB/GYN?"
> "What do piano lessons for the children cost here?"
> "How soon do we have to get driver's licenses and where do we go?"
> "Where can I find a good hairdresser?"

The questions go on and on, as do your opportunities to help your new family fit in as easily as possible.

Our survey respondents mentioned the schooling of their children as a major concern when they arrive in a new town. Good counsel on this matter is very helpful.

For families with preschool children, the providing of adequate child care is a lifesaver. Have you ever tried to open a bank account or stand in line for a driver's license while keeping track of a child or two? If so, you understand.

In California, and in other parts of the country as well, it seems impossible for a family to function without two cars. If that's true where you are and the new family has arrived from Duluth where one car sufficed, try to arrange a "loaner" to help out temporarily.

The Installation

For the new pastor or president, "installation" means the big formal ritual that starts his ministry. For his wife, "installation" has a more practical meaning of getting the washing and dryer working.

Colleges find it important to make a big fuss when a new president comes on campus. It helps get the smell of mothballs out of their academic gowns that they worked so hard to get and so seldom get to wear. Most churches do hold a welcoming reception after a service with a VIP speaker and a formal installation by the board.

I'm confident you will find an appropriate way to make a fuss over your new leader and to let him know how glad you all are that he came. That's great for him, but what about his spouse? The ladies of the organization should find a way to show their welcome to her also.

Christian organizations pay poorly, compared to secular positions that require the same years of preparation. In part, this explains why many wives work at such jobs as teachers, nurses and secretaries. As the new family arrives in town and settles in, the time may come when she needs or wants to be reemployed. Where does she start looking if she needs a secretarial job and lacks knowledge of the local business community? She could use the help of some knowledgeable parishioners to arrange introductions.

The Rush and the Quiet

Everybody wants to meet the wife of the new pastor or president. What is she like? How does she dress? Will she fit in? Does she expect to be a leader in various church groups? Is she one who ministers in her own right or is she just "his wife"? Seeking answers to these questions could be part of the getting-acquainted process as well as expressing a sense of hospitality. When the couple first arrives, this interest is sometimes expressed in more social opportunities than can be accepted.

> Dixie Bolinder says, "There is a big rush when you arrive. Everybody wants a piece of you in the beginning. That shuts down after awhile."

The wife of a new president of a parachurch organization provides another insight:

> It was great to be included in their social activities. We had to establish a new social circle. It would have been nice to have that continue. After the first time, I guess they just figured they didn't have to keep it up. I suppose it has something to do with your position. You know the saying, "It's lonely at the top." It is hard to have the ability to be included after the initial phase.

Perhaps your search committee can orchestrate some way to level out this social flood-then-drought sequence. A little thought and planning should make it happen. It would help to assure the new couple that declining some of those early invitations is acceptable, but then be sure to communicate with the congregation to make sure they understand that the new family is not being aloof or unfriendly.

Private time, that special interlude when you can be along or just with your spouse, is even more important when your new world is still swirling in your head. Those planning for the new couple's arrival would do well to encourage them to find this quiet time. The pressures of the new job and the unfamiliar surroundings can be intimidating and put heavy strains on family relationships. That is why all the mutually-nurturing times and experiences are especially needed at this time.

Finding Your Place of Service

As you would expect, many men who are Christian leaders have wives who are also gifted and able. However, as the leader is called to a new place of service, his wife often finds it difficult to regain the ministry role she had at their former place. My speculation about this involves these factors and you can probably add some more of your own:

- *Competition* If the new pastor's wife is an outstanding women's Bible teacher but one is already in place, she may not want to let anyone know for a while about her abilities.
- *Compensation*—If the church has a paid organist, secretary or other staff position and this is her area of excellence, arguments can arise over whether or not she should be paid.
- *Moving into the big leagues*—The premier soloist at First Presbyterian in Davenport, Iowa could find herself fortunate to be able to get into the choir at First Presbyterian in Hollywood, California.
- *The authority syndrome*—When it's the boss's wife that's involved, things can get sticky.

A thoughtful and thorough search committee should have learned early on what the gifts of the spouse were and what her hopes for continued ministry are. They should have seen a potential area of ministry for her before issuing the call and anticipated possible problems. Counsel may be helpful to her as she begins to fit in.

A more difficult situation is when the new pastor's wife has no leadership talents to offer or is so busy in a job that she has no energy or time to allow her involvement. Finding an acceptable role of nonservice can be very difficult, particularly if her predecessor was quite involved. A helpful search committee will do everything possible for such a wife to assure that her introduction makes clear that the church hired her husband, not her.

Christian Leaders with Husbands

Whatever problems a wife has in fitting in when her husband is called to a new ministry, the problems seem much greater for a male spouse following his wife. Thus far, not much is known on this subject because the Christian church has not yet elevated many females to major leadership roles. Research is needed in this area as well as with couples who are both employed in active Christian ministry, whether as a team or individually.

But whether that person is male or female, now that your long-sought president or pastor is heartily welcomed, officially installed, safely-housed and hard at work, I pray God's every blessing on you and your new leader. I wish you satisfaction in a job well done; I wish him a fruitful and rewarding ministry; and I wish you both a long and lasting relationship.

Notes
1. Both quotations by Dixie Bolinder and that by Margaret Ann Seiple in this chapter are used with their permission.

AFTERWORD:
Should You Seek
Outside Help?

Because I am a professional search consultant, you may expect me to encourage the use of a consultant to assist in the selection process for most Christian organizations. But I won't.

In selecting pastoral staff for a congregation, I am strongly against any outsider doing the search. All the sweat and pain of the search effort should be shared in by the search committee members as they refine the needs of the congregation and then seek qualified candidates. I suggest that, at most, a search consultant be used as an advisor to the search committee to help them set up a workable process and to coach them in using it.

Arguments Against

While the task of calling a pastor is often protracted and can be frustrating, it also can draw the committee together in a wonderful, mutually supportive way. Where a search committee cannot develop the needed vision, energy and cooperation to complete the task, I seriously doubt that they are worthy of a new leader.

If they, with such attitudes, were to try to delegate the search to a consultant, he would be sure to fail.

There is another reason not to use a search consultant—the cost. Most churches would find the fees of a good search consultant more than they could afford. Cut-rate consultants could prove even more expensive in the final analysis.

I have found nothing in Scripture and little in life's experiences to suggest that God blesses apathy or ignorance, even if we surround the effort with prayer and give it labels that sound very spiritual. A consecrated turkey is still a turkey.

Arguments For

Parachurch organizations or educational institutions, on the other hand, may find executive search consultants of considerable value, particularly at the most senior management levels. At the presidential level, particularly, the fees are better justified because the future of the whole organization is at stake.

The Christian college, Bible school or seminary has a board of trustees who are responsible for hiring a president. This is also true of an independent missions group or ministry, as well as of other parachurch organizations such as retirement homes, hospitals, broadcasting, publishing and other Christian group efforts. Such a board of directors/trustees would do well to consider using a search consultant under these circumstances:

1. If opposing political factions make agreement difficult;
2. If board members live in widely-dispersed locations;
3. If no board member has previously served on a search committee;
4. If members are too busy to commit significant chunks of time to the task;

5. If no person with the needed skills and time is available to serve as chairperson of the search committee.

The Holy Spirit and Consultants

If you are a rather traditional person, you may feel that the use of a consultant in choosing leaders for Christian institutions is obvious evidence of a lack of faith in God's guidance. Though I tend to be traditional in most matters, in this one I tend not to agree.

Years ago, in a simpler time, Christian organizations merely "trusted God" for adequate financial support, but today they have well-developed fund-raising abilities through the use of people with specialized skills. While abuses can arise in using such "professionals," the common practice now for Christian colleges and parachurch organizations is to have development (fund-raising) departments. When such professional fund-raisers are spiritually mature Christians who have developed the necessary technical skills and are guided by high stewardship principles, abuses can be avoided and much good can be done.

And so it is with the use of an executive search consultant. Such a person can broaden the number of qualified candidates the search committee will be able to consider. The Holy Spirit can operate just as effectively in the minds of the committee members whether a consultant found the candidates or they did it themselves. If the committee members themselves were not energetic or creative enough to find well-qualified candidates, that God will lead them to a decision assuring a satisfactory result is not likely.

A Consultant of Like Faith

I have found nothing in Scripture and little in life's experiences to suggest that God blesses apathy or ignorance, even if we surround the effort with prayer and give it labels that sound very spiritual. A consecrated turkey is still a turkey.

If any Christian organization is interested in using an executive search firm, be sure that the particular consultant who will be handling the search is someone who shares the essentials of the faith of the group to be served. I believe an evangelical

Christian group is in peril if it uses a recruiter who is not also evangelical.

By "essentials of the faith," I do not mean that the recruiter must be in agreement with the group's minor doctrinal points. However, if the ministry is devoted to foreign mission activities, the recruiter should be so committed to those tasks that he can be authentic and enthusiastic as he presents this particular ministry opportunity to candidates.

Professional Credentials

No professional credentials are needed to gain entry into the "profession." The executive search profession is immature and you need to be careful as you evaluate a firm you are considering. While you need to select a fellow Christian to help you, that should be only a preliminary qualification, not a determining one. You can find well-intentioned, sincere Christians who are in personnel work, who run employment agencies or who are in search firms who are nevertheless ill-equipped to help you. Remember: A consecrated turkey is still a turkey.

Guidelines

Here are a few guidelines if you are considering using a search consultant:

1. Avoid the firm that works on a contingent fee basis. Use a retainer-based firm.
2. Seek a firm that specializes in doing search work, not one that offers it as one of many services it offers. An exception is a firm with a highly-trained staff that does *only* search work as a distinct service.
3. In selecting a firm, speak with the person who would conduct the search, not someone else;
4. Seek information from the firm that assures you of their professional competence from both outside and inside the religious world. Being well-connected among Christians is not a fully reliable credential.
5. Talk to other organizations, such as ones like your own, that the search firm has previously served.

6. Interview several search firms before you choose.
7. Try to determine if the consultant's current work load allows sufficient attention to your needs.
8. Choose a consultant you feel you can trust and will enjoy working with.
9. Review again your internal candidates to be sure you are not missing someone who is promotable. If you are not sure, have the consultant evaluate the internal possibilities as well as those being considered from the outside.
10. If your search committee is not overwhelmingly supportive of using a search consultant, don't do it. As an outsider, the consultant hopes to work with a group that is not torn by internal politics, particularly on the point of his being a key part of the selection process.

You may find it helpful to read *Aiming High on a Small Budget: Executive Searches and the Nonprofit Sector* (see the bibliography). This small volume has some helpful material about selecting a search consultant even though it is not directed at the Christian community.

Christian Sources

Executive search is still quite new in Christian circles. The Christians in the search professions are still largely inexperienced in serving Christian organizations, so you may have difficulty in finding someone to assist you. As a starting point, you could see if various Christian service organizations know of a firm to suggest. Here are three such groups to query:

National Association of Evangelicals
450 E. Gundersen Drive
Carol Stream, Illinois 60187
Telephone: 312/665-0500

Christian Ministries Management Association
1930 Brea Canyon Road, Suite 170

Diamond Bar, California 91765
Telephone: 714/861-8861

MARC, a World Vision International ministry
121 E. Huntington Drive
Monrovia, California 91016
Telephone: 818/303-8811

Fees

Most executive search firms charge fees that are related to the compensation level of the position they will be seeking to fill. Most positions in Christian leadership circles have a salary scale so modest as to offer little motivation for the search firm to become involved, so the compensation level basis for fees is inappropriate.

The two common current practices for establishing fees are (a) hourly rates and (b) a fixed fee. The hourly rate method is the same means you use to pay your attorney or CPA. In this instance, however, you face a danger if an upper limit on the hours is not established in advance.

The fixed fee method simply says the search will cost a specific amount, an amount set by the consultant that reflects his estimate of the difficultly to complete the assignment. A variation of the fixed fee method is the setting of a minimum and a maximum fee with the final amount varying with how long the search takes. An early completion allows a minimum fee billing while a protracted search requires the maximum fee.

All search consultants require being reimbursed for the out-of-pocket expenses of the search such as travel, telephone, postage and so on. Be sure to have an understanding about expenses before the search commences.

Summary

If you are a church, you may wish to seek some counsel to advise your committee, but you should do the search yourselves.

Larger or more complex organizations may wish to consider

the use of an executive search firm for senior level officers. However, if you have the needed time, able committee members and a good chairperson, why not do it yourself?

APPENDICES

1. Church Profile Form (Reformed Church in America)
2. Church Information Form, Part IV, Pastoral Activities (Presbyterian Church, U.S.A.)
3. Church Information Form, Parts I, IA, II, III, V, VI (Presbyterian Church, U.S.A.)
4. Typical Work Week (of a minister)
5. Recruitment Profile (InterVarsity Christian Fellowship)
6. Minister's Profile Information Form (Baptist General Conference)
7. Letter to Prospective Candidate Whose Papers You Have Received
8. Letter to Prospective Candidate Whose Papers You Have *Not* Received
9. Letter Requesting Recommendation of Candidate
10. Sign-off Letter to a Candidate
11. Letter of Thanks to Sources
12. Offer of Employment Letter
13. Checklist for "Finalist" Candidates
14. Reference Check Form
15. Chart of the Events in a Search
16. Checklist for Concluding the Search
17. Postsearch Checklist
18. 1987 State Income Tax Rates

Appendix 1

CHURCH PROFILE FORM
REFORMED CHURCH IN AMERICA

1. NAME OF CHURCH _____
2. MAILING ADDRESS _____

   _____   TELEPHONE ___/___-____

              POSITION AVAILABLE   TODAY'S DATE

   _____   _____
        (Pastor, A.P., Youth Min., etc.)

3. PARTICULAR SYNOD _____   4. CLASSIS _____
5. CHAIRMAN OF PASTOR NOMINATING COMMITTEE _____

   ADDRESS _____

   _____   TELEPHONE ___/___-____

6. MEMBERSHIP   5 YEARS AGO   TODAY

          Active   _____   _____

          Inactive   _____   _____

7. AGE OF MEMBERS   % Under 20 ____;   % 20 - 34 ____;

   % 35 - 49; ____;   % 50 - 64 ____;   % 65 & Above ____

8. SPENDING   5 YEARS AGO   TODAY

   Total Spent for
   Congregational Purposes $_____ $_____

   Total Contributed
   to Benevolences $_____ $_____

   Percentage of total budget contributed by living donors:

          100 - 90% ____;   75 - 89% ____;   60 - 74% ____;

                 45 - 59% ____;   44% Or Less ____.

   Average yearly contribution per active communicant:

          $130 Or Less __ $130 - $180 __ $180 - $230 __

          $230 - $280 __ $280 - $350 __ $350 & Over __

9. SERVICE SCHEDULE   TIME   AVERAGE ATTENDANCE

                              _____   _____

                              _____   _____

                              _____   _____

10. CHURCH/SUNDAY SCHOOL   5 YEARS AGO   TODAY

    Enrollment   _____   _____

    Average Attendance   _____   _____

11. CHILDREN'S PROGRAM/ORGANIZATIONS (Age 12 or under) Describe briefly.

_____

_____

_____

_____

12. YOUNG PEOPLE'S PROGRAM/ORGANIZATIONS (Ages 13 - 21) Describe briefly.

_____

_____

_____

_____

13. ADULT GROUPS/ORGANIZATIONS (Age 22 or older)
     Use additional sheet if needed.

Name	Frequency of Meeting	Attendance
Name	Frequency of Meeting	Attendance
Name	Frequency of Meeting	Attendance
Name	Frequency of Meeting	Attendance
Name	Frequency of Meeting	Attendance
Name	Frequency of Meeting	Attendance

14. ECUMENICAL OUTREACH - In what ways have you co-operated with other
     churces in your community during the past year?

_____

_____

_____

_____

15. COMMUNITY OUTREACH - In what community programs or projects have you
     participated during the past year? (As an organization, not as
     individuals)

_____

_____

_____

16. LOCAL EVANGELISIM - What have been your three major methods of local
     evangelisim during the past year? (Use additional sheet if necessary)

     (1) _____

(2) _____

(3) _____

17. BUILDINGS - Are your buildings adequate for your present program? ____

Do you plan any capital expenditure during the next five years? _____

If yes, please explain briefly: _____

_____

Is there a mortgage indebtedness? _____ Amount? $_____

Of how long standing? _____ Annual rate of repayment _____

18. FINANCIAL ASSISTANCE - Do you receive financial assistance from Church Planning and Development? ____ Amount received last year $_____

19. PASTOR'S STUDY - In Church ____ In Parsonage ____ Other ____

Not Provided ____

20. STAFF - List all salaried staff in addition to the pastor:

_____Full time ____ Part time ____

_____Full time ____ Part time ____

_____Full time ____ Part time ____

_____Full time ____ Part time ____

_____Full time ____ Part time ____

21. CONSISTORY MEMBERSHIP - What method used in selecting members? _____

_____

List ages and occupations of present Consistory members:

Age	Occupation	Age	Occupation	Age	Occupation
__	_____	__	_____	__	_____
__	_____	__	_____	__	_____
__	_____	__	_____	__	_____
__	_____	__	_____	__	_____
__	_____	__	_____	__	_____
__	_____	__	_____	__	_____

22. Choose up to six of the following activities of the Christian Ministry which you consider to be most important as you look to the immediate future of your congregation. (Number them in order of preference)

(1) ___ ADMINISTRATION   (6) ___ PREACHING   (10) ___ WORK WITH COMMITTEES

(2) ___ PASTORAL CALLING (7) ___ COMMUNITY   (11) ___ PERSONAL
                                   ACTION   EVANGELISM

(3) ___ CHILDREN'S WORK   (8) ___ CONDUCTING   (12) ___ SMALL GROUPS
                                   WORSHIP

(4) ___ YOUTH MINISTRY   (9) ___ PASTORAL   (13) ___ MINISTRY TO
                                   COUNSELLING   FAMILIES

(5) ___ ADULT EDUCATION

23. In a typical week, how many hours do you expect your pastor to spend
    on top priority activities? (Please indicate for each of your six
    choices in question #22; include time for preparation of these
    activities.)

    FIRST CHOICE   1-5 ___; 6-10 ___; 11-15 ___; 16-20 ___; Over 20 ___
    SECOND CHOICE   1-5 ___; 6-10 ___; 11-15 ___; 16-20 ___; Over 20 ___
    THIRD CHOICE   1-5 ___; 6-10 ___; 11-15 ___; 16-20 ___; Over 20 ___
    FOURTH CHOICE   1-5 ___; 6-10 ___; 11-15 ___; 16-20 ___; Over 20 ___
    FIFTH CHOICE   1-5 ___; 6-10 ___; 11-15 ___; 16-20 ___; Over 20 ___
    SIXTH CHOICE   1-5 ___; 6-10 ___; 11-15 ___; 16-20 ___; Over 20 ___
    ALL OTHER DUTIES 1-5 ___; 6-10 ___; 11-15 ___; 16-20 ___; Over 20 ___

    How many hours would you wish your pastor to spend in study, prayer
    and meditation?

              1-5 ___; 6-10 ___; 11-15 ___; 16-20 ___; Over 20 ___

24. AGE LIMITATIONS: Check as many as you wish to consider.

    Under 30 ___; 31-40 ___; 41-50 ___; 51-60 ___; 61-65 ___;

    Over 65 ___

25. SPECIAL TRAINING/EXPERIENCE DESIRED (Describe briefly)

    _____

    _____

    _____

26. LANGUAGES - Should your pastor be fluent in any language other than
    English? _____ Please list and indicate importance:

    _____ Helpful ___ Essential ___ Primary Language ___

    _____ Helpful ___ Essential ___ Primary Language ___

27. NON RCA CLERGY - Are you willing to consider ministers who are not
    now serving in the Reformed Church? YES _____ NO _____

28. In our congregation . . .
         Few Many Most
    (1)___ ___ ___ have had up to twelve years of formal education.
    (2)___ ___ ___ have had some education beyond high school.
    (3)___ ___ ___ have a college degree.
    (4)___ ___ ___ have a graduate degree.

29. In our congregation . . .   (Number in order all which apply)

    (1) ___ there is a heavy concentration of scientists and engineers.
    (2) ___ there is a heavy concentration of farmers.
    (3) ___ there is a heavy concentration of business people.
    (4) ___ there is a heavy concentration of students and professors.
    (5) ___ there is a heavy concentration of industrial workers.

30. TYPE OF COMMUNITY SERVED

    (1) __ Rural, under 2,500   (4) __ Metropolitan-Suburban 50,000+

    (2) __ Town, 2,500 - 9,999   (5) __ Metropolitan-Inner City 50,000

    (3) __ Small City, 10,000-49,999 (6) __ Metropolitan-Urban, 50,000+

31. The income level of the people in our congregation tends to be:

    (1) ___ About the average for our community.
    (2) ___ Somewhat below the rest of the community.
    (3) ___ Somewhat higher than the rest of the community.

32. The last annual salary we paid a pastor was $_____.

    The average annual increase over the last three years was $_____ .

    The approximate annual value of benefits provided our pastor was:

    (1) _____ Pension (CAF or Other) (8) _____ Disability Insurance

    (2) _____ Major Medical Insurance (9) _____ Social Security

    (3) _____ Health/Hospital   (10) _____ Book Allowance
                      Insurance

    (4) _____ Life Insurance   (11) _____ Education Allowance

    (5) _____ Rental Value of   (12) _____ Utilities
                      Parsonage

    (6) _____ Housing Allowance   (13) _____ Other (Specify Below)

    (7) _____ Car Allowance

33. PARSONAGE - Current Market Value $ _____ Number of Bedrooms ____

34. RECORD OF LAST THREE PASTORS
          Name   Dates of Service

    _____   _____

    _____   _____

    _____   _____

35. Are there any particular Minister's Profiles you definitely wish to have sent? (OHR will send up 5 profiles at a time. You may return those which do not meet your requirements and request replacements.)

    _____

    _____

    _____

    _____   _____
    VICE-PRESIDENT, CONSISTORY   CLASSIS SUPERVISOR

Used by permission of the Office of Human Resources, Reformed Church in America, 475 Riverside Drive, Room 1808, New York, New York 10155.

CHURCH PROFILE FORM SELF-STUDY QUESTIONS

    When using the Church Profile Form, the following clarifications may be helpful. Numbers below refer to items on the Form. Questions are for group consideration during the self-study process.

        1-4 Self-explanatory.

        5   Self-study and Pastoral Search Committee, Pulpit Committee or whatever this committee is called.

6   See Minutes of the General Synod RCA (The Orange Book)

7   Tabulate from membership list. Do not guess or count only
     those who come on Sunday morning, since all members will be
     in some way part of the new minister's pastoral
     responsibility. Question: What do these statistics say
     about the program priorities of the congregation? What
     happens if the rate of past change is projected ten years
     into the future?

8   See figures in Minutes of the General Synod RCA for total
     spent for Congregational Purposes and contributed to
     benevolences. For the percentage contributed by living
     donors, do not calculate income from endowments, invested
     funds, or church-owned property.
     For the Average yearly contribution per active communicant,
     add the totals for Congregational Purposes and Benevolence
     Spending, subtract amount Not from living donors, then
     divide by number of active communicants. Question: What
     does this say about the stewardship emphasis in the
     congregation? Has it been sufficient, have stewardship
     programs been effective or is a different approach needed?
     If so, what kind?

9   Self-explanatory. Question: Is the trend up or down?
     Does style and form of worship meet the needs of some
     groups more then others? If so, which? Does this have any
     implications for the future of the congregation?

10   See Minutes of General Synod RCA, also Sunday School
     attendance records. Question: Is the trend up or down?
     How does this compare with trends in public school
     enrollment during the same period? Does the congregation
     need a different approach to the Christian education of
     children?

11   Self-explanatory. Question: Are parents given adequate
     support in their Christian education efforts at home? How?

12   Self-explanatory. Question: How do the young people on the
     committee feel about the emphasis the congregation is
     putting on youth work? Is there a budget item for youth?
     How much? Could a cooperative program with another church
     or churches offer more creativity?

13   Self-explanatory. Question: Have any of these groups
     outlived their usefulness? Do they each have a significant
     purpose? Which of these groups would you want to see
     started today if it did not already exist?

14-20 Self-explanatory.

21   See the Book of Church Order, Part I, Article 2, Section
     9.c (p. 16)

22-23 These are important questions, though admittedly they are
     difficult. However, each congregation does have definite
     expectations of its minister, even if these have not been
     articulated. Many open or hidden conflicts can be
     avoided if there is general agreement between pastor and
     congregation as to where the priorites should be focused.
     The amount of time to be spent in a particular activity
     should be directly related to its importance. Thus, if
     "Preaching" is a top priority item, no less than 11-15
     hours per week should be expected for the preparation of
     sermons. It is true that weeks will vary greatly, but
     imagine a so-called "typical" week. (Do not forget to add
     up the total number of hours expected!)

24   This item will be used for screening purposes. Those not
     checked will not be considered. Question: Is age really a
     significant factor, or are some people younger at 55 than
     others at 36? Would the congregation wish to eliminate
     every minister over 50 simply because of age? Some people
     in very demanding positions would be willing to serve a
     smaller congregation in the years immediately prior to

retirement, and can offer a wealth of experience, maturity, and a quality of leadership which the congregation might not be able to afford in the popular 31-50 age catagories.

25   Seminary training and standard or equivalent credentials of Reformed Church clergy are assumed. The item refers to requirement beyond this.

26   Self-explanatory.

27   Normally, files will be checked for RCA candidates first.

28   Check the item which applies to more people than any other.

29   Self-explanatory.

30   Self-explanatory.

31   Committee or consistory consensus is sufficient. Question: How should the salary of the minister be related to the answer?

32   Self-explanatory. Please use dollar figures.

33   Calculate as if it were to be sold today in present condition. Question: If a minister preferred a housing allowance, would it be wiser to sell the parsonage? See section on remuneration in the Handbook. (pp. 18-21)

34   Self-explanatory.

35   These will be sent immediately upon receipt of the completed Church Profile Form, thus they will not reflect a match with information contained in it.

Appendix 2

CHURCH INFORMATION FORM

PART IV - PASTORAL ACTIVITIES

PASTORAL ACTIVITIES

Below are 20 pastoral activities. You are asked to study the list and their definitions. Then determine your priority rating of these activities, in relation to your position, as follows: choose not more than six (6) of the activities on which you place the highest priority; then decide which (no limit) are lowest priority; the middle numbers represent degrees of importance. Each activity should have a circled rating by it.

		HIGH			LOW
A.	CORPORATE WORSHIP AND ADMINISTRATION OF SACRAMENTS (Pastor/Staff and Session work to develop a rich worship life, educating the congregation for meaningful participation.)	1	2	3	4
B.	PROCLAMATION OF THE WORD (The Word of God is preached with urgency and conviction, bringing it to bear on the changing needs of individuals, the community, and the word. High priority of pastor's time placed on sermon preparation.)	1	2	3	4
C.	SPECIAL WORSHIP SERVICES (Creative and innovative worship opportunities are provided, together with ways to increase understanding and celebration. Provision made for those who need or prefer other than the regular worship.)	1	2	3	4
D.	SPIRITUAL DEVELOPMENT OF MEMBERS (Pastor/Staff shares members' struggles regarding the Christian faith, with opportunity provided for individuals and groups to reflect on beliefs, concerns, doubts regarding Christian understanding of the spiritual dimensions of life.)	1	2	3	4
E.	CONGREGATIONAL HOME VISITATION (Church Officers and Pastor/Staff develop and carry out a systematic plan for visitation of the entire congregation with special attention to prospective members and those with special needs.)	1	2	3	4
F.	HOSPITAL OR EMERGENCY VISITATION (Those in hospitals or emergency situations are regularly visited; network developed to keep pastor and others informed of crisis situations; needs of ill or bereaved are met.)	1	2	3	4
G.	CONGREGATIONAL FELLOWSHIP (Emphasis is placed on developing fellowship, helping members to know one another; groups encouraged which give members the opportunity to love and support one another.)	1	2	3	4
H.	COUNSELING (A counseling program initiated for assisting those in and outside the Church; appropriate referrals made when needed.)	1	2	3	4
I	EVANGELISM (Pastor/Staff and congregation share faith in Christ as personal savior in total life style; seek to lead others within and outside the Church	1	2	3	4

to accept Jesus Christ; congregation is informed,
trained, helped to establish effective evangelism
program for the church.)

J. PLANNING CONGREGATIONAL LIFE   1   2   3   4
(Creative ideas and directions developed together
with the Session; many persons with appropriate
skills stimulated to become involved in services.)

K. INVOLVEMENT IN MISSION BEYOND THE LOCAL COMMUNITY   1   2   3   4
(Awareness of the Church's worldwide mission and
opportunities for corporate and individual
involvement; specific projects identified; persons
challenged to support, study and/or visit mission
programs on six continents.)

L. EDUCATIONAL PROGRAM   1   2   3   4
(Session and Pastor/Staff identify the educational
needs of persons of all ages and backgrounds,
developing programs to meet needs; church education
supported; educational goals are congruent with the
total mission of the Church.)

M. TEACHING   1   2   3   4
(Pastor/Staff accepts an active teaching role,
interpreting and teaching the Scriptures,
theological concepts, history of the Church and
current events; provides instruction for Church
Officers, educational leaders, confirmands and
new members.)

N. MISSION IN THE LOCAL COMMUNITY   1   2   3   4
(Concern for identifying social problems in the
community; work done with groups seeking solutions.
Time and skills committed to community groups.
Information and encouragement provided which
enables members to become informed and involved.)

O. ECUMENICAL AND INTERFAITH ACTIVITIES   1   2   3   4
(Involvement in ecumenical and interfaith
activities, with the congregation joining other
groups in presenting a united Christian witness
in the community.)

P. CONGREGATIONAL COMMUNICATION   1   2   3   4
(Two-way communication encouraged; information
gathered and shared that will assist problem
solving and decision making; varying opinions
elicited and all encouraged to listen to opposing
points of view.)

Q. ADMINISTRATIVE LEADERSHIP   1   2   3   4
(Pastor/Staff accepts appropriate administrative
responsibilities, in climate of delegated tasks
and shared leadership; volunteers and professional
staff encouraged to use their ideas and skills.
Work done developing accountability.)

R. STEWARDSHIP AND COMMITMENT PROGRAMS   1   2   3   4
(Session and Pastor/Staff develop a planned
stewardship education program to communicate
the financial needs of the local Church and
mission beyond the local church; congregation
challenged to commitment to Church's work.)

S. EVALUATION OF PROGRAM AND STAFF   1   2   3   4
(Systematic procedures used to evaluate programs
and staff performance in accord with goals and
objectives. Others trained to use these skills
Regular assessment and evaluation.)

T. RESPONSIBILITIES AND RELATIONSHIPS WITH PRESBYTERY 1   2   3   4
AND OTHER GOVERNING BODIES
(Value placed on balance between local church and
Presbytery/Synod/General Assembly responsibilities.

Congregation and Session know and are involved in
the work of the denomination.)

SPECIAL INTERESTS

We need a person who has special skills and interests in these areas.
[Please check no more than four (4).]

Early childhood	☐ (321)	Singles	☐ (326)
Elementary	☐ (322)	Middle Adult	☐ (327)
Youth	☐ (323)	Older Adult	☐ (328)
College	☐ (324)	Family	☐ (329)
Young Adult	☐ (325)		

Reprinted by permission of James E. Andrews, Stated Clerk, Presbyterian
Church (U.S.A.), 475 Riverside Drive, New York, NY 10115.

Appendix 3

PRESBYTERIAN CHURCH (U.S.A.)

CHURCH INFORMATION FORM

Part I - CHURCH PROFILE

A. Name and Address of Church: Date Forms Completed_____

                                         PIN_____ Date Church
                                                           Organized._____

                                         Position _____

                                         Synod_____

    Phone Number_(___)_____   Presbytery_____
            Area Code

B. If Yoked, indicate name(s) and address(es) of other churches.
    Attach a separate Church Profile for each church, AND Part 1A-
    Supplement for Yoked Churches.

C. Introductory Statement about the Church.

D. Introductory Statement about the Neighborhood
    This congregation serves a community or neighborhood which encompasses
    an area within _____ miles of the church.
    Total population of the town, city or rural area in which the church is
    located _____.
    Describe the area by checking any of the blanks below which apply:

    Inner City_____ Urban _____ Urban _____ Suburban _____ Town _____
                    (Downtown)   (Residential)

    Rural _____ College _____ Retirement _____ Recreational/_____
                                                  Resort

    Agricultural _____

E. Membership:
    Current Church Membership _____   Church Membership five years ago____
                                       (from Session minutes or Minutes
                                       of the General Assembly, Part II)

    Number of Members who are: Adult women _____ Adult men _____

    Youth _____

Average Attendance:

| Sunday Morning Worship _____ | Church School _____ | Sunday Evening Worship _____ | Mid-Week Service _____ |

Other Services of Worship (list and include approximate number of participants)

Racial composition of this congregation

How do these figures compare to the Racial Composition of the community?

F. Church School:
    Grades/Ages   Number enrolled   Materials Used

G. Organizations Within the Church (List Boards, committees of Boards, and number of members on each.)

    List other organizations, men's/women's groups, choirs etc.

    Has your Session adopted the "Commitment of Peacemaking?"
    Yes _____ No_____

H. Total Annual Budget for the current year, 19____ $_____

CHURCH INFORMATION FORM

PART IA - SUPPLEMENT FOR YOKED CHURCHES

A. Name and Address of each church/chapel.

B. What is the history of this yoked field? How long have the churches been yoked? Have they shared a pastor/staff person in the past? How do the people feel about it?

C. Distance between churches.

    Distance/driving time between churches: _____

    Total distance to be covered if more than two churches are involved:
    _____

Total driving time if more than two churches:_____

D. When does each church have Sunday Morning Worship? Hour?
    Times per month? Seasonal variations?

E. When does each church have Church School? Hour? Times a month?
    Seasonal variations?

F. Describe the schedule for any other regular activities such as choir,
    youth groups, women of the church. (List for each church, including how
    often and times of the day.)

G. Describe the activities in which the churches join together.

CHURCH INFORMATION FORM

PART II - NARRATIVE INFORMATION

If the session or the commitee has done a Mission Study before beginning to
work on these forms, you may use information from that report in place of
this section. However, the denominational offices, in the interest of good
stewardship, will not circulate more than five pages of narrative
information.

A. THE CHURCH AND THE NEIGHBORHOOD
    1. The Church
        a. Describe your congregation as it might look to a person leading
            worship. Include information about members and visitors, their
            racial makeup, ages, sex.

        b. As you consider the membership of your church what
            occupations, educational levels, etc., are represented?

        c. Where do members live in relation to the location of the
            church?

        d. Are there seasonal events which alter the routine of your
            church's program?

        e. Describe the church's properties including the manse. Comment
            on any major needs or plans concerning buildings.

    2. The Neighborhood
        a. Describe the area served by your church. Specify the radius
            used. For example, where is it located geographically? What
            is the population of the town, city or village in which the
            church is located? How far is the church from the nearest
            commercial center? What is the church's ministry to the area?
            What other churches (Presbyterian and other) are within the
            area?

        b. What lifestyles, housing patterns, employment and community or
            economic concerns are in evidence? How does the membership of
            the congregation compare with the neighborhood with regard
            to these factors?

        c. What educational, cultural and medical facilities are available
            in your community or nearby?

B. PROGRAMS

The following questions are designed to augment information given in Part 1. Select at least three or four of the questions below and use them to expand on items mentioned on pages one or two.

1. Describe your church's corporate worship life, including regular Sunday and week-day services, special worship services and programs. Were any changed in the past ten years? How?

2. Describe the eduational programs in which your church is involved. What facilities are available? Include adult education, leadership development and week-day programs. When do these take place?

3. Describe some programs and organizations which have been/are most meaningful in your church's ministry?

4. What skills and style of pastoral leadership would best enable your congregation and the person filling the position to work together in fulfilling the mission of your church? Is this different from the past?

5. What mission causes, both denominational and non-denominational does your church support? Include amounts or percentages of total budget.

6. Describe the functioning of governing boards of your church. For example, is there a committee structure? How frequently does each board meet? What is the usual amount of time expected of pastoral staff? How much time is the pastor/associate pastor expected to give to this work?

C. VIEWPOINTS

1. Comment on your understanding of some of the major issues which your community and the world will be facing in the coming decade. Do you think your church should respond?

2. In consideration of the goals of the church, what changes would you, the congregation, hope to experience within the next five years?

CHURCH INFORMATION FORM

PART III - POSITION DESCRIPTION

Name of Church/Agency _____ Date _____

City/State _____ P.I.N. _____

(Complete this information exactly as it appears in Part I.)

This Position Description is to be used in conjunction with the Church Information Form dated _____.

Title of Position: (Check One)

___ Pastor-Solo (No other full time   ___ Associate Pastor (Called by the
           professional staff)   Congregation and the
                                                        Presbytery)

___ Pastor--Head of Staff (Staff   ___ Lay Professional (eg. Educator,
        includes at least one other   Musician, Administrator--
        professional)   not neccessarily ordained)

___ Co-Pastor (Two or more pastors
        are called to share
        pastoral role)

Other _____

A. Responsibilities: (For what specific tasks, assignments, program areas will this person have responsibility? Be sure to compare this Section with C. below for consistency.)

B. Working Relationships: (List persons, boards and/or committees with whom this person will work most closely. Describe any special relationships to community or presbytery structures.)

C. Pastoral Activities: (Of the activities listed in Part IV, which are in the column labeled "High"?)

D. Describe the characteristics and qualifications needed in a person who would fill this position:

E. Staff: (In addition to name and position, indicate, using the codes shown, whether the person is Full-Time (FT); Part-Time (PT); Man (M); Woman (W); Racial/Ethnic other than Caucasian (RE).

F. Evaluation and Review: (Who is responsible for performance reviews and salary reviews? How often are they held?)

G. Salary and Benefits: (What is the minimum cash salary? Is it negotiable? What major benefits are also provided? What type of housing and housing allowance is offered?)

H. Is this a full-time position? _____ If not, how much time will the position require each week? What other employment opportunities exist for a person filling this position?

I. Date position became vacant? _____

By whom was it last filled? _____

What is that person doing now? _____

CHURCH INFORMATION FORM
PART V - FINANCIAL INFORMATION

A   Church Budget

1.   Total Amount Budgeted for this year $_____

2.   Financial Statement for the last completed fiscal
     year. (19__)

INCOME		EXPENDITURES	
Pledges:	_____	Operating Expense:	_____
Offerings/gifts:	_____	Debt Repayment:	_____
Presbytery:	_____	Benevolences:	_____
Other Income:	_____	Other Expenditures:	_____
TOTAL INCOME	$_____	TOTAL EXPENDITURES	$_____

3.   Special Offerings and Contributions

     Amount Received in Special Offerings
     during last year: TOTAL $_____

     Amount contributed to non-denominational
     causes last year: TOTAL $_____

4.   Does your church have a system for receiving pledges?
     _____ Yes _____ No

     If your church does receive pledges,

        How many pledges were made for the current fiscal year? _____

        What is the total amount pledged for the current year? $_____

           If necessary, you may attach further information about your
           church budget.

B. Terms of Call

1.   Salary and Housing   Fixed Amount $_____

     a. Cash Salary   or

                              Negotiable Range $_____ to $_____
                                               Minimum   Maximum

     b. Housing

         1) Is a Manse provided? ____ Yes ____ No

         2) If a Manse is provided, what is the
             fair rental value used? $_____

         3) If Housing Allowance is provided,
             what is the yearly total? $_____

         4) Utility Allowance $_____

     c. TOTAL of Salary and Housing (Add all $_____ to $_____
         items under a. and b.)   Minimum   Maximum

2.   Benefits (Use both minimum and maximum salary
     figures to compute.)

a. Pension/Annuity
    Payments made to:
        Pension Plan (Include Major Medical) $_____
            or
        Annuity $_____

        Other Pension or Annuity_____ $_____

b. Payments made for additional medical $_____
    insurance

c. Other (Additional Insurance, Social
    Security, etc.) $_____

d. TOTAL of all benefits (Lines 2a, b, and c) $_____

        TOTAL of Cash, Housing and Benefits $_____ $_____
                                               Minimum   Maximum

3. Reimbursed Expenses

    a. Auto/Travel Expenses $_____

        How Paid? _____

    b. Continuing Education $_____

        How Paid? _____

    c. Book Allowance $_____

        How Paid? _____

    d. Other Allowances (explain) $_____

        TOTAL PACKAGE $_____ $_____
                                               Minimum   Maximum

Vacation Time _____

Continuing Education Time _____

CHURCH INFORMATION FORM

PART VI - INFORMATION FOR DENOMINATIONAL OFFICES

A. Maximum distance from which you wish to consider ministers.

    Within   Within   Within
    400 Miles _____   800 Miles _____   1200 Miles _____   Unlimited _____

B. Experience Required: Please indicate the total number of years of
    experience which the person you seek must have by marking one of the
    following choices.

                Recent seminary graduate
                with no full time church   _____ At least four to ten years
        _____ experience   experience

                At least one to three   _____ More than ten years
        _____ years experience   experience

C. If you require that this experience be in a particular setting, such as
    type of community, kind of position, or size of church, please indicate
    it.

D   Special Qualifications: Occasionally there are situations in which
special skills, such as foreign language fluency, special
certification, advanced academic work, or simply life experience may
be required or helpful. Please list such skills below, and we will
attempt to suggest persons with these gifts.

E.   Optional Information for Opportunity Lists. In some cases, up to two
typewritten lines of narrative information about a church or community
may be included when the position is listed. If you choose this option
to emphasize the special nature of your church or position, please use
the space below.

F.   About the Pastor Nominating Committee.
These forms were prepared by the Pastor Nominating Committee, which
consists of:

_____ Adults; _____ Men;   _____ Session   _____ Racial/Ethnic
                                   Members;   Persons.
_____ Youth;   _____ Women;

Name and Address of the Chairperson

Telephone (_____)_____
            Area Code

Name and address of another person who can provide information about
this position.

Telephone (_____)_____
            Area Code

G.   EQUAL EMPLOYMENT OPPORTUNITY

"The Presbyterian Church (U.S.A.) shall give full expression to the
rich diversity within its membership and shall provide means which will
assure a greater inclusiveness leading to wholeness in its emerging
life. Persons of all racial ethnic groups, different ages, both sexes,
various disabilities, diverse geographical areas, and different
theological positions consistent with the Reformed tradition shall be
guaranteed full participation and access to representation in the
decision making of the church." (G-4.0403)

"(The Committee on Ministry) shall provide for the implementation of
equal opportunity employment for ministers and candidates without
regard to race, ethnic origin, sex, age or marital status. In the case
of each call, it shall report to the Presbytery the steps in this
implementation taken by the calling group." (G-11.0502f)

"...Care must be taken (by the Pastor Nominating Committee) to consider
candidates without regard to race, ethnic origin, sex or marital
status." (G-14.0502)

FORM OF GOVERNMENT PRESBYTERIAN CHURCH (U.S.A.)

See also: Form of Government G-10.0102m, G-11.0502d, G-13.0201b.
--------------------------- ---

Every Presbytery Committee on Ministry is to inform each Pastor Nominating
Committee of its constitutional obligations and how it might assure
fairness in the calling process.

Has the Presbytery's Committee on Ministry thus counseled with the Pastor
Nominating Committee regarding Equal Employment Opportunity?
Yes _____ No _____

Each Pastor Nominating Committee is expected to undertake its search for a
minister in a manner consistent with the good news that in the Church
"... as many of you as were baptized into Christ have put on Christ. There
is neither Jew nor Greek, there is neither slave nor free, there is neither
male nor female; for you are all one in Christ Jesus." (Galatians 3.27-28)

Has the Pastor Nominating Committee affirmed to the Presbytery Committee
on Ministry its intention to follow the Form of Government in this regard?
Yes _____ No _____

Indicate what steps your Pastor Nominating Committee intends to take to
implement the Form of Government in this regard:

_____

_____

H. ENDORSEMENTS

Parts I-VI of this form have been reviewed and found to be a fair and
adequate description of the church/agency and position.

Signed:_____ Date _____
(Chairperson, Pastor Nominating Committee)

Signed: _____ Date _____
(Clerk of Session)

Personnel Referral Services is hereby authorized to refer Personal
Information Forms.

Signed:_____ Date _____
(Representative of Prebytery's Committee on Ministry)

Please print or type name/title _____

Address _____

City/State/Zip_____ Phone_____

For the Presbytery of _____ Phone_____

Appendix 4

Typical Work Week

Monday - Friday

8:00 A.M. - 12:00 noon--in office.

The work at the office would be as follows (not in any particular order).

1. Prayer.

2. Bible study and sermon preparation.

3. Read poetry, literature, history, current events, religious trends write articles, etc.

4. Formulate ideas for the church program. Have suggestions for committees.

For me, personally, I find that 15 hours on sermons and 5 hours on a Bible study minimum. This comes to over 20 hours each week.

During the office hours there should be no phone calls before noon, except emergencies. All calls can be made to the parsonage or the church secretary, if such exist. Urgent messages can be relayed from these sources.

12:00 P.M. - 2:00 P.M.--lunch

2:00 P.M. - 4:00 P.M. (Tues., Wed., Thurs. only)--visitation to hospitals, sick families where the husband works nights, etc.

6:00 P.M. - 10:00 P.M. (approx.), Tuesday, Thursday evenings--office hours for counseling at the church. Those with problems can call any time of day or night, and I will come. However, to keep counseling meaningful and effective, these hours will be kept for consultation in my office. When there is no counseling on these evenings, I will be out visiting.

6:00 P.M. - 10:00 P.M. (approx.). Wednesday evenings--prayer service, committees. If all meetings were held on Wednesdays (Deacons, first Wed. of month, etc.), then I could be at a meeting each week and still do my work adequately. The pastor would be at each scheduled meeting of the major committees.

Monday, Friday, Saturday evenings--will be spent with my family, and I am very anxious to maintain this responsibility to them.

Sunday-- duties obvious.

Such a schedule is flexible but only when demands to adjust are meaningful. Total expected work hours per week: 55.

Appendix 5

Recruitment Profile

A Description of the Position of

PRESIDENT

AND CHIEF EXECUTIVE OFFICER

of

INTERVARSITY CHRISTIAN FELLOWSHIP

Madison, Wisconsin

THE ORGANIZATION: In 1939 InterVarsity Christian Fellowship began on the campus of the University of Michigan as a student group desiring to share their faith in Jesus Christ with other students. From that modest start InterVarsity has grown to now being active on 750 U.S. campuses in all 50 states. There are 780 InterVarsity employees who staff the programs and provided support services for 24,600 students during 1986-1987.

The 1987-1988 consolidated budget will be $26 million and 1986-1987 revenues exceeded $23 million. Revenues slightly exceeded expenses during 1986-1987 and overall InterVarsity is financially healthy. Long term debt is negligible and total assets exceed $11 million. During 1986 headquarters office operations were consolidated from several buildings to a newly refurbished building, still located in Madison, Wisconsin. The new location will take care of InterVarsity's needs for some years to come, even with reasonable growth.

Over its 47 year history InterVarsity has had a distinguished ministry and garnered the enthusiastic support from a broad spectrum of evangelical Christian churches, organizations and leaders. In addition to campus ministry, InterVarstiy has developed a substantial impact on foreign missions through the triennial Urbana conferences they have held continuously since 1948. The 1987 Urbana Missions Conference is expected to draw a capacity group of students, as usual, 18,000 in number.

Other missions activities of InterVarsity include missions counseling of students interested in service opportunities and overseas training camps. During 1986 these summer camps were held in Europe, Hong Kong, Kenya, the Middle East, the Philippines and Nigeria.

InterVarsity has a camping ministry at three locations. In Michigan's upper Peninsula, near Colorado Springs and on Catalina Island off the California coast, a variety of programs are offered to help students learn to grow in the walk of faith.

Nurses Christian Fellowship, Theological Students Fellowship, Faculty Ministries and Black Campus Ministries are additional special ministries of InterVarsity. IVCF is an active member of the International Fellowship of Evangelical Students.

In the world of ministry through print and media InterVarsity is quite active. InterVarsity Press, a well respected Christian publisher had sales of over $4 million last year. Twenty One Hundred Productions uses their multi-media tools to communicate the gospel message to college students and churches. Bible and Life training seminars, which have been offered for over twenty years, had 3500 students participating last year.

Since its founding by C. Stacy Woods, IVCF has been led by Charles Troutman, Dr. John Alexander, James McLeish and Gordon McDonald. Most recently, Tom Dunkerton became president of the organization in early 1987 when Gordon McDonald resigned. He had recently retired from an outstanding business career and he moved into the presidency from his previous role as InterVarsity Board member. He will serve as president until his replacement is selected.

Madison, Wisconsin, the home of InterVarsity, is a lovely community that offers a high quality of life but without the high costs found in many areas. However, Wisconsin taxes are rather high. Heavily influenced by the presence of state government offices and the University of Wisconsin, the educational and cultural opportunities are excellent. Recreational opportunities abound through the state.

THE POSITION: PRESIDENT AND CHIEF EXECUTIVE OFFICER

RESPONSIBILITIES   Reporting to the Board of Trustees, the President is responsible for directing all the operations of InterVarsity under the policy direction of the Board. The President will establish the goals and objectives of InterVarsity, obtain Board approval for them and assure their successful implementation. Also, the President will serve as a member of the Board of Trustees.

PROFESSIONAL
QUALIFICATIONS: This leadership role requires the balancing of managing the business aspects while nurturing the staff so that they minister to students in a caring and productive way as they challenge students to have life commitment to Jesus Christ. Many Christian leaders will have the spiritual depth, pastoral heart and proclaiming skills needed for this position. Far fewer leaders will also possess the managerial abilities and experience that are required to direct this complex organization. Only a few seem likely to add to the spiritual leadership and the managerial experience the desired background of significant involvement in the academic world. Nevertheless, that is the preferred background that is being sought. It is desirable that candidates have had involvement with IVCF in their past.

The President of InterVarsity Christian Fellowship will be in contact with a variety of people outside of the organization. This person should be able to deal effectively with:

- College and university students;
- Christian faculty on secular campuses;
- College and university administrators;
- Theological seminaries and other educational institutions from which IVCF staff may be recruited;
- Missionary leaders whose influence and support will enhance IVCF's effectiveness in mission work;
- Denominational and parachurch leaders whose understanding and cooperation will assist the ministry of IVCF:
- Foundations and key individual donors who offer significant suppport;
  Corporative executives

EDUCATION:

Candidates must have a baccalaureate degree. Graduate degrees would be a welcome additional credential and an earned doctorate would enhance acceptance in the academic world. Whether through theological studies or through less formal means, candidates must have a knowledge of God's word and the ability to expound it before groups.

In addition, candidates should be informed of trends and issues of note in the evangelical world.

MANAGEMENT
EXPERIENCE:

With the diverse ministries to students, media productions and publishing activity, IVCF is a complex organization with a $26 million budget, a sizeable management group in Madison and 780 employees serving in widely dispersed locations, the management tasks will challenge even the experienced administrator.

Candidates should have a background of significant management experience in a complex organization of substantial size. This experience could have been obtained in business, the academic world, parachurch organizations or denominational management positions. Other possibilities could be health care, publishing or broadcasting, whether with for-profit firms or non-profit. Appropriate size would be a budget exceeding $10 million, more than 300 employees, with two or more activities/ministries and having two or more levels of managers.

It is essential that candidates have a record of leading an organization in the reaching of significant goals. Maintaining an organization's good health is a solid achievement but a better credential for this position would be achieving significant growth, diversification of ministries or revitalizing an organization.

FUND RAISING
ACTIVITIES:

College presidents and heads of parachurch organizations are well acquainted with this aspect of their leadership role. At IVCF too, it is an important responsibility and could involve up to 20% of the President's time. The Development Department conducts the day-to-day fund raising activities and sets the stage for the President to make key contacts with foundations, corporations and major donors. A background of successful fund raising activities is preferred but not essential. In its absence, it is essential that this person have both the willingness and the ability to communicate the goals and needs of IVCF in a winsome, persuasive fashion. Candidates should be committed to presenting IVCF as an opportunity for significant stewardship.

COMMUNICATIONS
SKILLS:

The position requires the abilities to communicate effectively both in writing and orally to groups and one-on-one. However, it is not necessary that this person be one of the outstanding speakers/preachers/teachers in the country.

PERSONAL
QUALITIES:

THE SPIRITUAL
DIMENSION

IVCF wants a leader with both spiritual maturity and vitality. Someone is needed who articulates their personal relationship with Jesus Christ clearly and enthusiastically so as to provide a role model for the IVCF staff. This candidate should express their faith in a warm, caring way characterized by an openness to associates and a commitment to the tasks of evangelization and foreign missions. This person's Christian walk will involve an intimate knowledge of scripture and an active prayer life

Whatever the church background of candidates, it should
be acceptable to the mainstream of evangelical
Christians. Candidates should be comfortable in
fellowshipping with a broad range of Christian brothers
and sisters, not just a narrow sector of fellow
believers. Also, this person must be an active member
of a local fellowship and committed to the vital role
of the local church.

THE ACADEMIC
SETTING

IVCF ministers in a secular and intellectual
environment. Candidates for President of IVCF should be
able to function well in this diversity and have the
intellectual alacrity to respond well to it. An
awareness of American university life and IVCF ministry
on campus would be a valuable asset for candidates.

PERSONALITY

This position requires someone who is accomplished at
selecting and developing their staff rather than trying
to do it all personally. Candidates should be proven
team builders who have pride in the accomplishments of
their subordinates. Hopefully this will include a
record of developing and encouraging women and ethnic
minorities in responsible leadership positions. They
will have a participatory leadership style but have the
courage to make tough decisions and handle
confrontation when it is necessary. To use a well-worn
phrase, IVCF requires a servant-leader.

This person will be emotionally stable and have a
healthy level of self confidence, but aware of
dependence on the Lord for guidance personally and for
IVCF.

Although a demanding job, being President of IVCF
allows the incumbent an acceptable personal and family
life if the responsibilities are managed well. It
requires a spouse who is supportive and shares "the
call" to IVCF, even if not actively involved in
ministry. The President will need to travel
substantially, though it is not possible to say how
much. The family at home should be able to function
well despite this travel requirement. The higher
priority of family responsibilities must be carefully
balanced with leadership duties to handle successfully
this position.

AGE AND
HEALTH

Candidates should be old enough to have the experience
and maturity that has been described. However, they
should be young enough and in sufficiently good health
that they can reasonably expect to have ten years of
service in this position, Lord willing. This position
will require a high energy level.

THE REWARDS:

InterVarsity has a unique place among Christian
ministries and leading it offers a singular opportunity
to serve the Savior. Impacting young people during
their college years is a ministry requiring a high
level of creativity and presents a strategic return on
the investment of labors for Christ. Suitable
candidates for this position will view with excitement
this service opportunity.

An appropriate compensation package will be devised to
meet the needs of the person selected. While the
compensation will be attractive when compared to most
Christian organizations, candidates from the business
world will recognize that the Christian service
opportunity is the primary attraction. In addition to
the salary, a variety of fringe benefit programs are
provided to offer life and medical insurance and
pension benefits

STATEMENT OF FAITH: The President will be required to accept this doctrinal statment:

1) The unique Divine inspiration, entire trustworthiness and authority of the Bible.

2) The Deity of our Lord Jesus Chirst.

3) The necessity and efficacy of the substitutionary death of Jesus Christ for the redemption of the world, and the historic fact of His bodily resurrection.

4) The presence and power of the Holy Spirit in the work of regeneration.

5) The expectation of the personal return of our Lord Jesus Christ.

George D. McKinney, Jr.
Pastor
St. Stephen's Church of God in Chris
San Diego, California

Chester T. Youngberg
Retired
Corvallis, Oregon

Allen W. Mathis, Jr.
Professional Corporate Director
Mathis & Mathis, Inc.
Montgomery, Alabama

E. Kenneth Nielsen
Manager/Operations
New England Power Exchange
Southwick, Massachusetts

Donald L. Powell
President
Auto Research Labs, Inc.
Chicago, Illinois

James W. Reapsome
Executive Director
Evangelical Missions
Information Service
Wheaton, Illinois

David W. Scott
Vice President
Georgia Duck and Cordage Mill
Scottdale, Georgia

Appendix 6

BAPTIST GENERAL CONFERENCE

MINISTER'S PROFILE INFORMATION

Last Name   First Name   Middle initial

Address: Street   City   State   Zip   Phone

Present Church Membership   City   State   Zip

I. BASIC BIOGRAPHICAL DATA

1. Date of birth_____ Married _____ Date of Marriage_____
                  year/month/day

2. If married, give spouse's full (maiden) name _____

3. Give names and year of birth of your children.
    Name_____ Date___ Name_____ Date___

    _____ _____   _____ _____

    _____ _____   _____ _____

4. Give brief summary of your conversion experience. _____

    _____

    _____

    _____

5. Education. List school, degree and year obtained. (College and higher.)
    School   City and State   Degree   Date of Degree

    _____ _____   _____   _____

    _____ _____   _____   _____

    _____ _____   _____   _____

    _____ _____   _____   _____

6. Are you bilingual? _____ If so, what languages? _____

7. Have you been divorced? _____ Has your spouse been divorced? _____
    If yes, explain _____

    _____

8. Training, major interest of spouse, attitude toward your vocation.

    _____

    _____

    _____

9. Please check the position or position(s) listed below in which you are
interested.

_____ Pastor   _____ Minister of Music

_____ Associate Pastor   _____ Minister of
                                               Administration

_____ Minister of Christian Education   _____ Other _____

_____ Minister of visitation

If other than pastor, note Section III, 4 and 5.

II. PROFESSIONAL EXPERIENCE

1. Are you licensed? _____ Date _____ Ordained? _____

   Date of ordination _____ By which church _____

2. List experience in churches giving length of service and position. If
part-time, indicate. If Seminary student, give primary experience
during your field service or intern.

Church	City and State	Position	From Month Year	To Month Year

3. Have you had experience in new church development? _____ If so,

   comment. _____

   _____

   _____

4. Give information concerning your present or most recent ministry,
including the membership and financial growth pattern. If more than
six years, use last six.

Year your ministry began	19___	19___	19___	19___	19___	19___
Membership						
Budget General						
Missions						
Building						

Give reasons for growth or lack of growth _____

_____

_____

_____

5. Other ministry: Missionary service, chaplaincy, etc (Specify type of service, place and length.)

_____

_____

_____

6. List secular work which has helped in preparation for your ministry.

_____

_____

_____

7. What cultures (rural/innercity/suburb/black/white/etc.) do you work in best? Comment. _____

_____

_____

III. PERSONAL EVALUATION

1. Which of the New Testament gifts do you claim for yourself?

_____

_____

_____

2. What do you conceive your task as a minister to be? _____

_____

_____

3. Appraise yourself in the following functions of ministry.

   Preaching. (How do you feel about its importance in relationship to your ministry? What type do you do most of - topical? expository? etc.

   _____

   _____

   _____

   _____

   Teaching. (What methods do you use? What age group are you best with?)

   _____

   _____

   _____

   _____

   Evangelism. (What place does it have in your ministry? What methods have you used?)

   _____

_____

_____

_____

<u>Visitation.</u> (How important do you feel it is in relation to your ministry?)

_____

_____

_____

<u>Counseling.</u> (Evaluate your abilities.)

_____

_____

_____

<u>Administration.</u> (List type of administration in which you have been involved. Evaluate your abilities.)

_____

_____

_____

Rank these six functions of ministry in the order of where you feel most competent. (#1-most competent, #6-least competent.)

1._____   4._____

2._____   5._____

3._____   6._____

What has been your time allotment for these functions in your present ministry?

_____

_____

_____

4. Describe your expectations and philosophy of team relationships within a multiple staff. Identify whether your perspective is from that of the senior pastor or one of the team members.

_____

_____

_____

_____

5. If you are desiring a position on a multiple staff other than the senior pastor, indicate your areas of interest and your approach in each of the following aspects of team ministry.

A. Christian Education _____

_____

_____

B. Youth Ministries _____

_____

C. Music _____

_____

D. What adult ministries do you desire? _____

_____

E. What position title do you desire? _____

_____

F. How much preaching do you desire to do? _____

G. For how long do you anticipate this kind of position bringing
    personal and professional satisfaction to you?

_____

6. Comment briefly on the following items in relationship to yourself.

Program for personal devotional life _____

_____

Program for continuing education, (include professional conferences,
courses audited or taken for credit)

_____

List periodicals which you read regularly for enrichment _____

_____

What are the most significant three books which you have read within
the past year?

_____

_____

Health or physical limitations _____

_____

What do you do to maintain your physical health? _____

_____

How do you spend your leisure time? _____

_____

What do you feel is your greatest personal strength? _____

_____

What do you feel is your greatest personal weakness? _____

_____

7. List three things which indicate your greatest satisfaction in your present or most recent ministry._____

_____

_____

List three things which indicate your greatest disappointment in your present or most recent ministry. _____

_____

_____

8. Have you published any books, articles for professional journals, etc? If so, list._____

_____

_____

9. Please state briefly your theological position _____

_____

_____

_____

_____

_____

IV. AFFILIATIONS

1. Are you in agreement with the Baptist General Conference's "Affirmation of Faith"? Comment. (See enclosed instruction sheet.)

_____

_____

2. What is your attitude toward the educational and missionary programs of the Conference?

_____

_____

_____

3. Will you support and promote as a partner the Baptist General Conference and the district ministries. Comment.

_____

_____

_____

4. Why do you wish to serve in the Baptist General Conference? _____

_____

_____

5. Do you prefer a specific geographical area for your ministry at this point in your life? Specify.

_____

_____

6. List denominational, community and other activities or organizations in
    which you have participated in recent years _____

    _____

    _____

    _____

V. FINANCES

1. Salary requirements. Indicate what you feel is necessary for you at
    this point in your ministry and family needs. (These can either be
    itemized or given in a total figure.)

    _____

    _____

    (This information will not be disclosed to a church, but its purpose is
    to give the Placement Committee a guideline as to the feasibility of a
    church being able to provide what you feel are basic needs.)

2. Are you enrolled in the BGC Retirement Plan? _____

3. Do you have another plan? _____ If so, name_____

4. Are you enrolled in the BGC Health Plan? _____

5. If not, other health plan _____

VI. REFERENCES

List names and addresses of three individuals--one of whom served as a
leader in recent church experience.

_____   _____

Name   Complete address and phone number

_____   _____

_____   _____

Please enclose a photo of yourself. Family members can be included if you
wish.

                                   Date: _____

                                   Signature: _____

Is there any information contained in this questionnaire that you do **not**
wish shared with churches to whom you may be suggested as a possible
candidate? If so, indicate by section number below.

Additional Comments:

Appendix 7

LETTER TO PROSPECTIVE CANDIDATE
WHOSE PAPERS YOU HAVE RECEIVED

Dear Rev. Ambruster:

Wallace Memorial Church is beginning a search for Senior Pastor to replace Dr. David Bidwell, who will soon be retiring. Your papers have been received from the denominational offices and we are pleased to have the opportunity to review your credentials as our search process begins. Your background appears to meet our selection criteria and we would like to explore with you the possibility of your serving the Lord here as our pastor.

I have enclosed for your review a packet of information concerning our church and community. About two weeks from now I will be calling you to inquire whether you have interest in discussing this ministry opportunity. I look forward to answering any preliminary questions you may have at this time.

It is an exciting process to explore who will be our next spiritual leader and we look forward to getting to know you.

Cordially,

Chair, Search Committee

(Send letter to home address, not church office, on your church's letterhead.)

Appendix 8

LETTER TO PROSPECTIVE CANDIDATE
WHOSE PAPERS YOU HAVE NOT RECEIVED

Dear Rev. Scanton:

Wallace Memorial Church is beginning a search for Senior Pastor to replace Dr. David Bidwell, who will soon be retiring. Your ministry has come to our attention and we would like to explore with you whether our church is a place where God might lead you to serve.

I have enclosed for your review a packet of information concerning our church and community. About two weeks from now I will be calling you to inquire whether you have interest in discussing this ministry opportunity. I look forward to answering any preliminary questions you may have at that time.

As we begin our search process, a number of interested potential candidates have come to our attention, as you would expect. In addition, we are reaching out to a few persons, such as you, who appear to us to be particularly appropriate for our needs and who seem likely to extend the vision of ministry the Lord has given us.

I look forward to our telephone chat, getting acquainted and sharing with you about Wallace Memorial Church.

Cordially,

Chair, Search Committee

(Send letter to home address, not church office, on your church's letterhead.)

Appendix 9

LETTER REQUESTING RECOMMENDATION OF CANDIDATES

Dear Dr. Blenford:

Alfred Durning University is undertaking a search for a new president to replace Dr. Durning, III., who will shortly be made Chancellor of the University. Your broad range of acquaintances in Christian higher education prompts me to contact you and inquire if you have any names to suggest as potential candidates.

Enclosed is material about Alfred Durning University, as well as a description of the position of president and a list of the selection criteria we are using. I am sure you know quite a bit about us and the enclosures will outline a number of the distinctives that we cherish as an institution committed to serving Christ.

Thank you for your assistance.

For His Kingdom,

Appendix 10

SIGN-OFF LETTER TO A CANDIDATE

Dear Rev. Tiddelman:

You will recall that we were recently in touch with you concerning your interest in the need of Calvary Community Church for a senior pastor. Your papers were one of a large number that we have carefully and prayerfully reviewed in light of our selection criteria.

We have now focused our attention on a few candidates whose qualifications and experience seem to more closely fit our needs than yours appear to do. Your interest in our church is appreciated and we wish you God's leading and blessing as you seek where He would have you serve.

Cordially,

Appendix 11

LETTER OF THANKS TO SOURCES

Dear Dr. Spansler:

Some time ago we were in touch with you as our church began our search to find a new senior pastor to replace Rev. Roger Chadberry, who was retiring. We sent the letter to a number of people who we felt were well positioned t be of assistance and who we felt would be helpful. Many were and are very grateful.

Our search is now completed and our church is thrilled with the certainty that we were led to select Rev. Nancy Aines to minister to us. Her skills, interests and experience match well our needs and the vision we have for ministry. She will be joining us September 1st.

Thank you for your interest, concern and help.

In His service,

Appendix 12

OFFER OF EMPLOYMENT LETTER

Dear _____:

On behalf of the Exuberant Fellowship, I am delighted to extend you an invitation to join us as our Senior Pastor. The vote of the congregation to call you was overwhelmingly positive and the Search Committee and Board were unanimous. We believe God has clearly spoken to us that you are to lead us in the coming years.

We have discussed with you the duties of Senior Pastor and a copy of the written position description is attached. Hopefully you can conclude your present ministry without undue haste and be able to join us on August 1st, after a period of vacation. If it is possible, we would like to have your reply to this offer by the end of this month and your guidance as to when we could share the happy news with our congregation, if you accept.

Our compensation offer is as follows:

        Salary: $30,000
        Housing allowance: $12,000
        Car allowance: $2,000
        Book allowance: $500
        Study leave annually: 2 weeks
        Vacation: 4 weeks per year until 10 years service,
                   5 weeks for 10 to 15 years and 6 weeks for subsequent years

To encourage you to use your vacation annually, it does not accrue from year to year unless approved by the Board in advance.

    Medical/hospitalization: Fully paid for the entire family

    Life insurance: $50,000 with your contribution as provided under
                     our group plan.

    Sick leave: Four weeks per year is allowed with the hope that this is
                     an unduly generous provision. Sick leave can be accrued
                     from year to year up to a maximum of six months.

    Pension Plan: Your annual pension plan contribution to our
                     denominational pension fund will be paid by the church

It is our intent that at ten-year intervals of service you be provided a six-month sabbatical leave to be used for purposes of ministry enrichment However, the Board reserves the right to approve your request at that time in light of the prevailing circumstances.

You will be responsible to the Board of the church who will annually review your performance and your compensations. Our relationship with you is a continuing one that requires either party to give a 90 day notice of intent to terminate it.

We look forward to many years of your ministry with us under God's blessing. Nevertheless, we regard it as prudent to provide a basis of ' separation payment in the unlikely event of your being terminated by the Board. Until you have completed ten years of service, you would receive six months of salary, housing allowance, insurance coverage and pension plan contributions. After ten years, the same coverage would be provided for one year.

It is normal practice for a minister to receive an honorarium to perform weddings, funerals, etc. Such income is in addition to your salary, as is income from occasional speaking engagements or writing. The Board will work out with you an arrangement concerning your absences from the pulpit for outside preaching, including denominational commitments. We would expect your consultation with the Board before you make continuing time commitments that occur during your usual hours of ministry to the church.

Please let me know of any questions you have on any of these points. A letter offering employment can be viewed as impersonal and even legalistic because of its content, but let me assure you of our sense of expectancy and excitement as we anticipate where God can lead us with you as our pastor.

We look forward to your acceptance.

_____
Chair, Search Committee

_____
Chair, Church Board

Appendix 13

CHECKLIST FOR "FINALIST" CANDIDATES

Date

____ Received dossier

____ Obtained indication of interest

____ Degrees verified

____ Reference checks done

____ 1.

____ 2.

____ 3.

____ 4

____ 5.

____ 6.

____ Visit made to his church

____ Listened to sermon tapes

____ Interview with search committee

____ Second interview, with wife.

____ Search committee post-interview evaluation

____ Determining candidate's continuing interest

____ Decision by search committee to present to board/congregation or dismiss

____ Credit check made

____ Physical examination

Appendix 14

REFERENCE CHECK FORM

<u>CONFIDENTIAL</u>

Candidate: Rev. Danny Wynder

Source:

Relationship to the candidate:

Known for how long?

What are his best ministerial skills?

How good are they?

In what areas of ministry is he weak or in need of developing and how weak
is he in these areas?

Where would you rate him overall in comparison with other ministers who
have his years of experience?

What does his congregation think of his ministry?

Is the congregation divided in its opinion?

Is there anything negative about his personal or professional life that
could harm his next ministry?

Please describe his family and how they relate to the church. Is the
marriage solid?

How would you describe his health and energy level?

Please describe his leadership style and how he relates to the board.

What have been his most significant achievements and failures in his
present ministry?

Would you want him (again) as your pastor/president?

What have I not asked that is important to know, as we consider him as our
leader?

Date_____

Appendix 15

CHART OF THE EVENTS IN A SEARCH

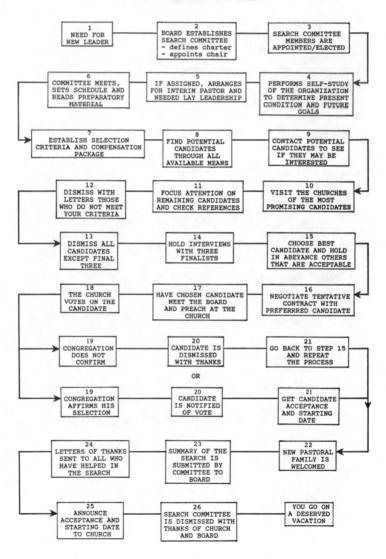

Appendix 16

CHECKLIST FOR CONCLUDING THE SEARCH

DATE

_____ Congregation or board votes acceptance.

_____ Offer letter sent to selected candidate.

_____ Acceptance received.

_____ Welcome letter sent to new leader and spouse.

_____ Announcement of acceptance and starting date made to congregation.

_____ Remaining candidates dismissed with thanks.

_____ Approval obtained from denominational authorities, if needed.

_____ Letters of thanks sent to sources and others who assisted in the search process.

_____ Letters of thanks sent by board chair to search committee members.

_____ Final report made to board by search committee chair.

_____ Arrangements made with treasurer to begin paying salary, reimburse relocating expenses, etc.

_____ Files are destroyed on all candidates not selected.

Appendix 17

POSTSEARCH CHECKLIST

Here are a variety of duties that should be taken care of at the conclusion of the search effort.

1. Assure that copies of the employment contract (letter) is in the possession of the board and the new leader.

2. Have a written acceptance of the offer in the hands of the board.

3. Let the candidates that were not selected know the results of the search and your appreciation for their interest.

4. Send notes of thanks to helpful references who helped you gather data on your candidates.

5. Prepare a report for the board that highlights the good and bad things the committee did. This report would guide subsequent search committees.

6. Dispose of all material on candidates who were not selected.

7. Send note of thanks and the search results to all the helpful sources who suggested possible candidates.

8. Send note of thanks to those who have been your advisors during the search, such as denominational executives, seminary officials, etc.

9. Have someone appointed to follow up on details of the new leader's move and any other needed assistance. This person should be the contact person for the newly selected leader until a relationship is established with the board.

10. The search committee is dismissed by the board.

Appendix 18

1987 STATE INCOME TAX RATES

STATE	RATE	at	INCOME LEVEL
Alabama	5%		over $6,000
Alaska	None		
Arizona	8% minus $497		over $14,196
Arkansas	7%		over $25,000
California	11%		over $28,790
Colorado	None		
Connecticut	None		
Delaware	8.2% 8.8%		$30-40,000 over $40,000
D. of C.	10%		over $20,000
Florida	None		
Georgia	6%		$70,000
Hawaii	9.75% 10%		$28-40,000 over $40,000
Idaho	7.0% 8.2%		$15-40,000 over $40,000
Illinois	2.5%		of Federal Income Tax
Indiana	3.4%		of Federal Income Tax
Iowa	8.8% 9.98%		$30-45,000 over $45,000
Kansas	9%		over $25,000
Kentucky	6%		over $8,000
Louisiana	4%		$10-40,000
Maine	9.2% 10%		$21-32,000 over $50,000
Maryland	5%		over $3,000
Massachusetts	5%		All
Michigan	4.6%		of Federal Income Tax
Minnesota	9%		over $21,000
Mississippi	5%		over $10,000
Missouri	6%		over $9,000
Montana	10% 11%		over $10,500 over $48,100
Nebraska	5% 5.9%		$22-45,000 over $45,000
New Hampshire	None		
New Jersey	2.5% 3 5%		$20-50,000 over $50,000

New Mexico	5.9% 6.9% 7.7% 8.5%	$24-36,000 36-48,000 48-64,000 over 64,000
Nevada	None	
New York	8.5%	over $23,300
North Carolina	7%	over $10,000
North Dakota	9.3% 10.67% 12%	$25-35,000 35-50,000 over $50,000
Ohio	4.506%	$20-40,000
Oklahoma	6%	over $15,000
Oregon	9%	over $5,000
Pennsylvania	2.1%	All
Rhode Island	2.3-4.0%	of Federal Income Tax
South Carolina	7%	over $10,000
South Dakota	None	
Tennessee	None	
Texas	None	
Utah	7.75%	over $7,500
Vermont	25.8%	of Federal Income Tax
Virginia	9.75%	over $14,000
Washington	None	
West Virginia	4.5% 6% 6.5%	$25-40,000 40-60,000 over $60,000
Wisconsin	6.93%	over $20,000
Wyoming	None	

Rates based on adjusted income for joint returns. Differing rates in some states for investment income.

Source: State Tax Review, Commerce Clearing House, December 15, 1987.

BIBLIOGRAPHY

A*IMING High on a Small Budget: Executive Searches and the Nonprofit Sector*. Independent Sector, Washington, D.C., 1986.

Blair, Charles and Sherrill, John. *The Man Who Could Do No Wrong*. Wheaton, IL: Tyndale House, 1982.

Boykin, John. *Circumstances and the Role of God*. Grand Rapids, MI: Zondervan Publishing House, 1986.

Drucker, Peter F. *The Effective Executive*. New York: Harper & Row, Publishers, Inc., 1967.

———— *Innovation and Entrepreneurship: Practice and Principles*. New York: Harper & Row, Publishers, Inc., 1986.

Dunker, Marilee Pierce. *Days of Glory, Seasons of Night*. rev. ed. Grand Rapids, MI: Zondervan Publishing House, 1984.

Friesen, Garry and Maxson, J. Robin. *Decision-making and the Will of God: Alternative to the Traditional View*. Portland, OR: Multnomah Press, 1980.

Gilley, Wade J., et al. *Searching for Academic Excellence: Twenty Outstanding Colleges and Their Leaders*. New York: Macmillan Publishing Co., 1986.

Griffin, E. "Confessions of a Pulpit Committee." *Leadership*, Summer 1984.

Ketcham, Bunty. *So You're On the Search Committee*. Washington, D.C.: Albvan Institute, 1985.

Kubler-Ross, Elisabeth. *Questions and Answers on Death and Dying*. New York: Macmillan Publishing Co., 1974.

Leadership: A Practical Journal for Church Leadership. Published quarterly by Christianity Today, Inc., 465 Gundersen Drive, Carol Stream, Illinois 60188.

Mead, Loren B. *Critical Moment of Ministry: A Change of Pastors*. Washington, D.C.: The Alban Institute, 1986.

_____ *Evaluation: Of, By, For and To the Clergy*. Washington, D.C.: The Alban Institute, 1977.

On Calling a Pastor. New York: Vocation Agency, Presbyterian Church (U.S.A.), 1984.

ABOUT THE AUTHOR

Robert W. Dingman and his wife, Jan, live in Westlake Village, California. For over 25 years he has been an executive search consultant and he has been president of his own firm, Robert W. Dingman Co. since 1979.

He is a graduate of Houghton College in western New York state, where he met his wife. He did graduate studies at Boston University, George Washington University and Rutgers University. For 10 years he served on the board of trustees of Whitworth College, Spokane, Washington, and he now is on the board of directors of Mission Aviation Fellowship. Active in the hospice movement that assists the terminally ill, he has served as patient-care volunteer, board member, president of the board and fund-raiser for Hospice of the Conejo. He is an elder in Emmanuel Presbyterian Church in Thousand Oaks, California. The Dingmans have three grown children and two grandchildren.

In recent years his efforts have included serving Christian parachurch organizations. He has done more than 10 presidential searches for Christian organizations, both large and small. These clients include World Vision International, Mission Aviation Fellowship, InterVarsity Christian Fellowship and CRISTA Ministries. However, most of his executive search practice remains in the world of business.

Mr. Dingman is active in the leadership of the California Association of Executive Recruiters, as well as the activities of the Association of Executive Search Consultants. His firm has been included several times on the roster of "Leading Fifty Search Firms in the U.S."